PARTIMENTO AND CONTINUO PLAYING
IN THEORY AND IN PRACTICE

D1453386

*This ninth publication in the series
"Collected Writings of the Orpheus Institute"
is edited by Dirk Moelants*

PARTIMENTO AND CONTINUO PLAYING

IN THEORY AND IN PRACTICE

Thomas Christensen

Robert Gjerdingen

Giorgio Sanguinetti

Rudolf Lutz

COLLECTED WRITINGS OF THE

ORPHEUS

INSTITUTE

Leuven University Press

2010

CONTENTS

PREFACE

This volume is a collection of essays based on lectures given at the 4th *International Orpheus Academy for Music Theory* in 2006. The theme of this Academy was *Music and Theory: Thoroughbass in Practice, Theory, and Improvisation.* Hence the point of departure was not "Music Theory" as such, but the interaction between music theory, music history, performance practice, aesthetics and related sciences. This multidisciplinary approach, with the accent on the interplay between music performance and music theory is reflected in the contributions to this book.

Thomas Christensen, in his contribution, shows how the development of tonal harmonic theory went hand in hand with the practice of thoroughbass. Both Robert Gjerdingen and Giorgio Sanguinetti focus on the Neapolitan tradition of *partimento.* Gjerdingen addresses the relation between the realization of *partimenti* and contrapuntal thinking, illustrated by examples of contrapuntal imitation and combination in *partimenti*, leading to the "*partimento-fugue*". Sanguinetti elaborates on the history of this *partimento-fugue* from the early 18th until the late 19th century. Rudolf Lutz, finally, presents his use of *partimenti* in educational practice, giving examples of how reviving this old practice can give new insights to composers, conductors and musicians.

Dirk Moelants

THOROUGHBASS AS MUSIC THEORY

Thomas Christensen

Thoroughbass is typically understood today as a largely practical discipline of music, one in which the keyboardist learns to play (or "realize") the chords encoded in figured-bass notation in some stylistically-appropriate manner.[1] It is not surprising, then, that the vast majority of didactic literature used to teach thoroughbass in the 17th and 18th centuries emphasizes this mechanical aspect of chord realization. It is true that this practice is one that may at times blur the boundaries of compositional creativity, or musical *poesis*. (The skills needed for the realization of the thoroughbass and those for compositions were closely related in the Baroque musical world; indeed for many pedagogues, they were viewed as complementary disciplines.)[2] But thoroughbass nonetheless remained a quintessentially practical skill of music, even if it was a skill demanding a strong "poetic" component of creativity and taste.

It may come as a surprise, then, for us to learn that thoroughbass was also deeply implicated in the speculative music theory of the *Zeitalter des Generalbasses*, as Hugo Riemann designated the period from 1600 to 1750. That is to say, the many challenges of realizing a figured bass for a performer of that time also presented explanatory challenges to speculatively-minded theorists. The pedagogical mnemonics by which figured-bass was taught to young musicians became a surprisingly powerful instigation for remarkable developments in the area of tonal music theory. At the same time, some of the theoretical formulations of these speculative writers were reciprocally applied within the realm of thoroughbass pedagogy.

---

1. While I will henceforth refer to the keyboard in discussing thoroughbass pedagogy, it should be remembered that it was also possible to realize chords on a strummed instrument such as a guitar or theorbo in some contexts.
2. In a recent article, I have traced in some detail the history of the complex interrelationship between thoroughbass and compositional pedagogies. See Thomas Christensen, "*Fundamenta Partiturae*: Thoroughbass and Foundations of Eighteenth-Century Composition Pedagogy", in: Thomas F. Kelly & Sean Gallagher (eds.), *The Century of Bach and Mozart: Perspectives on Historiography, Composition, Theory and Practice*, Cambridge Mass. 2008, pp. 17–40.

In the following essay, I want to explore this mutually symbiotic relation between through-bass practice and speculative music theory.[3] We will see that one major figure will loom large throughout this story: the French composer and music theorist, Jean-Philippe Rameau (1683–1764). This should not be surprising, since Rameau was without question the most important innovator in the development of modern harmonic theory. What is perhaps less well known, though, is the importance thoroughbass practice played as a catalyst to his radical theorization of tonal practice. That is the story I wish to tell in this essay, a story entailing four differing chapters of tonal music theory.

1.

CHORDAL IDENTITY

One of the most salient features of thoroughbass is that it asks us to think of music in terms of a series of successive chords. These chords are encoded in a notation of Arabic numerals (or "signatures") that indicate their interval structure above a continuo bass line, usually disregarding octave compounding and doublings. Through the medium of the thoroughbass, composers and performers alike were accustomed to hear most music as a series of these chords sutured through appropriate voice leading.

Of course there were a wide variety of chords to learn for any student, providing a serious pedagogical challenge for teachers and performers alike. A continuo player was faced with a potential blizzard of differing figures in reading a continuo-bass line. To teach these, teachers would collect these many signatures into a comprehensive listing or "table". In Example 1, we see one such table of signatures, this one from Johann Mattheson's important treatise on thoroughbass from 1735, *Kleine General-Bass Schule*.[4] The signatures are ordered — as was typical of the day — based on ascending inter-

---

3. I have elsewhere explored the epistemological distinctions between "practical" and "speculative" modes of music theorizing. See Thomas Christensen, "Genres of Music Theory", in: *Towards Tonality: Aspects of Baroque Music Theory*, Leuven 2007, pp. 9–39.
4. Johann Mattheson, *Kleine General-Bass Schule*, Hamburg, 1735.

val content: all chords containing an interval of a second (whether major or minor) were listed first, those containing a third followed, those with a fourth after that, and so on.

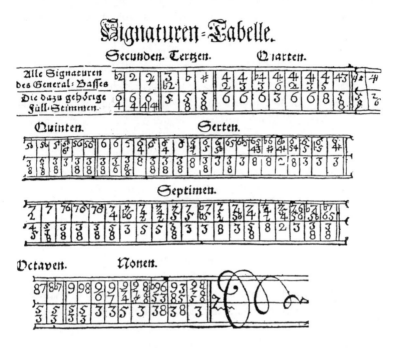

Example 1. A "Signature Table" from Johann Mattheson, Kleine General-Bass Schule, *Hamburg 1735, p. 136.*

One can imagine the paralysis which might beset a young student faced with this abundance of chordal figures. Of the 70 figures itemized in Mattheson's table (and the number could be more or less, depending on the treatise one consulted), the student would theoretically have to learn the fingering of each and every chord above potentially any scale degree in any key. This is not even to worry about proper voice-leading between the chords, let alone any stylistically-appropriate embellishment or diminution. Clearly some means of pedagogical simplification was called for.

The first step came when a few thoroughbass teachers realized that many of these chords could be learned and played as variants of one another. The right hand of a keyboardist could grip a single "perfect" harmony (that is, a major or minor triad) against which the left hand (bass note) might move, producing irregular "positions" of the triad, or a variety of non-triadic harmonies. The French theorist and composer Michel de St. Lambert explained this simple trick as follows in his treatise of 1707:

> Those who are learning Accompaniment usually have more difficulty understanding and remembering by heart figured chords than [they do] perfect chords. But it is easy to make this less difficult, by pointing out that when a [bass] note has several figures that assign to it an unusual chord — this chord (though unusual for that particular bass note) is often the perfect chord of another [bass] note. When an UT, for example, is figured with a 6, the chord denoted by 6 on UT is the perfect chord on LA; if it is figured with four and six 6/4, this is the perfect chord on FA; if it is figured with 7, or with 7/5, or with 7/5/3, this is the perfect chord on MI, etc. In order, therefore to give the reader all possible assistance on the above matter, I am going to teach him how to imagine the majority of dissonant chords indicated by these figures as perfect chords.[5]

From this perspective, then, it was easy to think of both 6/3 and 6/4 chords as derivative of the perfect triad. We must be clear, though, and not forget that St. Lambert did not speak of these derivative chords as "inversions" let alone "equivalents". Given the 17th-century theoretical perspective within which he was writing, any such notion of "inversional equivalence" would have been inconceivable. After all, the crucial elements in defining a signature were the kinds of intervals one found above a given bass note, not the pitch-class content of the collections. It would have been nonsensical in St. Lambert's mind to think of a chord containing two imperfect consonances (such as a 6/3) to be considered equivalent to a chord with a perfect and imperfect consonance (5/3), let alone a chord consisting of a dissonance and an imperfect consonance (6/4).

Clearly, St. Lambert's was only a clumsy but useful rule of thumb for helping the student to realize some figures. But it is also clear

---

5. Michel de Saint-Lambert, *Traité de l'accompagnement du clavecin*, Paris 1707; trans. John S. Powell, *A New Treatise on Accompaniment*, Bloomington 1991, p. 23.

that something like this rule of thumb led Rameau to formulate his famous principle of inversional identity in 1722. We know from Rameau's own testimony that it was precisely the practical problem of signature realization in the context of the thoroughbass that led him to develop — and formalize theoretically — his notion of chordal inversion.[6] The key insight Rameau brought to St. Lambert's short cut was that of a *son fondamental* — a fundamental sound that could also be understand as the generative root of the harmony. (Here Rameau was relying upon a speculative tradition of interval generation upon the monochord — a tradition that would have been foreign to St. Lambert's practical outlook.)[7] It was this generative root that would essentially define a chord, so that no matter which note of the chord appeared in the bass, its fundamental sound remained unchanged. Most significantly, though, the *son fondamental* may be transposed by an octave to any inner voice and still retain its name and function as the foundation and generator of harmony. This is because of the unique quality of the octave, whose notes retain their identity no matter in what register.[8]

Thus, a C Major ("perfect") triad on C had the same generative root as did the 6/3 chord on E, and a 6/4 chord on G. More audaciously, Rameau made the same argument for seventh chords. Thus a 6/5/3 chord was seen as the first inversion of a root-position seventh chord, 6/4/3 the second inversion, and 6/4/2 the third inversion,

---

6. Rameau first worked out the notion of inversional equivalence in his *Traité de l'harmonie* of 1722. But we know through a study of his early manuscripts that he had worked out an informal notion of the theory much earlier. See Thomas Christensen, *Rameau and Musical Thought in the Enlightenment*, Cambridge 1994, pp. 51–61. The *Traité de l'harmonie*, it should be noted, consists of four books; the first two constitute the theoretical explanation and illustration of the theory of chordal generation and the fundamental bass, respectively, while books 3 and 4 deal with the application of this theory to the disciplines of composition and accompaniment, respectively.
7. For more on Rameau's development of the *son fondamental* and its origins in traditional monochord theory, see Christensen, *Rameau and Musical Thought*, pp. 90 ff.
8. "... cette Octave n'y a d'autres proprietez que celles qui luy sont communiquées par le Son fondamental dont elle est engendrée, ou pour mieux dire encore, que c'est toûjours le même Son qui se transpose dans son Octave ou dans sa replique, ou encore qui se multiplie, si l'on veut, pour déterminer de tous côtez des intervales particuliers à chaque Son qu'il a engendré, sans alterer neanmoins les proprietez qui sont tombées en partage à ces Sons engendrez dans la premiere comparaison qui a dû en être faite d'abord avec ce Son fondamental." (*Traité de l'harmonie*, p. 8).

all because they possessed the same generative fundamental. Even chords of the 9th or 11th were seen as seventh chords at heart, with bass notes "supposed" below the seventh chord. (So, for example, a 9th chord built above C was actually viewed by Rameau as a seventh chord on E, with the C an added note "supposed" below the true root of E.)[9] We can see in Example 2 a table from the fourth book of Rameau's *Traité* in which this idea is clearly illustrated. The right hand (*Main droite*) grips a seventh chord on five differing scale degrees, below which the left hand (*Main gauche*) plays six differing notes that produce either chords of inversion, or chords of supposition.[10]

Now this principle of chordal inversion is so familiar to most of us today that it is easy to overlook how revolutionary it was for its time, and how it was directly in response to the challenge of thoroughbass pedagogy that it was formulated. Of course Rameau went beyond this to enunciate a more rigorous (if not entirely consistent) theory of chordal identity and generation. (While it would be too digressive to detail this here, we might simply point out that in his earliest formulations, Rameau grounded his theory of harmonic genera-

---

9. In the same way a chord of the 11th (or a suspended fourth) can be analyzed as a seventh chord, with a supposed root placed a fifth below the actual root. While Rameau's theory of supposition came into a great deal of criticism as unintuitive, there is an underlying logic to it when one puts it in the context of the fundamental bass, discussed further on in this essay. In any case, it is clear that the original concept of supposition is congruent with the practical heuristic that guided his initial formulation of chordal inversion: triads and seventh chords can be seen as the foundational structure of most every figured-bass signature, to which certain notes might be added or altered.

10. "Si l'on peut donc ajoûter un cinquiéme Son à l'Accord de la Septiéme, ce ne peut être qu'au dessous et non au dessus, ou pour lors ce Son ajoûté supposera le fondamental qui se trouvera immediatement au dessus de luy; de sorte que nous ne chercherons point le principe dans l'Octave de ce Son ajoûté, mais dans celle du Son fondamental qu'il suppose; et c'est ainsi que nous pourrons rapporter exactement la progression de ces derniers Accords à celle des précédens. L'Accord de la Septiéme qui s'y trouve toûjours depuis le Son fondamental supposé, pourra se renverser de même qu'auparavant; mais le Son ajoûté ne pourra jamais changer de lieu, il occupera toûjours le grave, pendant que les autres profiteront du renversement, dont ils peuvent participer entr'eux comme étant contenus dans les bornes prescrites par l'Harmonie; ces derniers suivront leur progression naturelle dans le Mode qu'ils representeront, et le Son ajoûté s'évanoüira, en se réünissant avec eux; de sorte qu'il ne peut être regardé que comme surnumeraire, puisque l'Harmonie fondamentale y subsiste toûjours sans luy, et que la progression des Accords n'y est point alterée." (*Traité de l'harmonie*, p. 74).

tion using the venerable tool of the monochord, while later in his life, he invoked a more "natural" origin in the harmonic overtone series—the *corps sonore*.)

E X E M P L E

Example 2. Derivation of various chords of inversion and "supposition" from 5 differing seventh chords. Jean-Philippe Rameau, Traité de l'harmonie, *Paris 1722, p. 379.*

Now this principle of chordal inversion is so familiar to most of us today that it is easy to overlook how revolutionary it was for its time, and how it was directly in response to the challenge of thoroughbass pedagogy that it was formulated. Of course Rameau went beyond this to enunciate a more rigorous (if not entirely consistent) theory of chordal identity and generation. (While it would be too digressive to detail this here, we might simply point out that in his earliest formulations, Rameau grounded his theory of harmonic generation using the venerable tool of the monochord, while later in his life, he invoked a more "natural" origin in the harmonic overtone series — the *corps sonore.*)

But no matter how grounded, the pedagogical value of this theory was clear. Not only would the notion of inversional derivation help a student learn to realize a signature quickly on the keyboard, it could also help in the voice leading. Consider this example: By traditional contrapuntal theory, a perfect fourth above the bass was an undisputed dissonance needing to be prepared and resolved downward by step. Yet this was not the normal practice for the 6/4/3 chord, where the fourth seemed to behave like a consonance. (What was worse, in this same chord, it was the consonant third that usually "resolved" downward by step.) With the theory of the fundamental bass, this paradox could be easily explained. For it turns out that this chord is but a second inversion of the dominant seventh chord, and the "third" actually represents the seventh that needs to resolve (while the "fourth" doubles the fundamental sound of the chord, and thus need not resolve). By knowing which note of a chord was derived from the essential dissonance of the seventh, the student would be ready to "resolve" that note correctly no matter its position above the continuo bass.

It is not surprising that Rameau's theory of chordal inversion proved so popular to pedagogues; it proved to be an eminently practical heuristic for realizing the thoroughbass. Johann David Heinichen recognized immediately its value when he was in the midst of publishing his mammoth *Der Generalbass in der Composition* of 1728, and he hastily emended his text by incorporating notions of chordal inversion (*verwechseln* or *verkehren*).[11] Consider the table

---

11. See Joel Lester, *Compositional Theory in the Eighteenth Century*, Cambridge 1992, pp. 55–56.

reproduced in Example 3, from what is arguably the most important and widely-consulted manual of the thoroughbass published in Germany in the 18th century, David Kellner's *Treulicher Unterricht im General-Bass*.[12] We can see in Kellner's table that four varieties of seventh chord are all laid out in inversional rotations. (Kellner — just as with Heinichen — says nothing about the roots or generative fundamental of these chords, incidentally, suggesting how easy it was to disentangle this concept from that of chordal inversion.)

Example 3. Inversions of Seventh chords from David Kellner, Treulicher Unterricht im General-Bass, *Hamburg 1732, p. 92.*

---

12. David Kellner, *Treulicher Unterricht im General-Bass*, Hamburg 1732.

So far we have only spoken of chords derived from inversions of
the triad or seventh chord (and incidentally of the 9th or 11th). But
what of the many other dozens of chords in Mattheson's signature table given in Example 1? Most of these other chords, it will
be quickly realized, are ones whose characteristic attributes stem
from the inclusion of non-harmonic tones (products of suspension,
appoggiatura, pedal point, or anticipation). In fact, though, each of
these could be accommodated within Rameau's system simply by
analyzing them as alterations or deflections of the simple triad or
seventh chord (and their various inversions). In this way, the basic
claim of Rameau—that there are two fundamental chord types
in all music, one the consonant triad, and the other the dissonant
seventh—remains valid. Some version of this "two chord" thesis
was adopted by countless thoroughbass pedagogues in the later 18th
century. I will let Johann Philipp Kirnberger stand as representative
of this perspective, although any number of other figured-bass teachers might equally well have been chosen.

70 ⁂

§. 171.

Consonirende ⁴⁄₃ Accord.

Beym consonirenden ⁴⁄₃ Accorde, können eben so wohl, wie beim Dreißlang und
Sexten-Accord, eine, zwei und drei zufällige Dissonanzen vorgehalten werden, die nach
ihnen stehende consonirende Töne, in welchen die Dissonanzen sich auflösen, zeigen auch,
was für Töne denen noch fehlenden Consonanzen zukommen müssen, die man sogleich bei
denen zufällig dissonirenden Intervallen anzuschlagen hat, als:

6 —		7 6		6 —		9 8		mit einer zufälligen
5 4		4 —		3 4		6 —		Dissonanz
8		8		8		4 —		

mit 2 Dissonanzen.   mit 3 Dissonanzen.

*		*		*		*		*
7 6		7 6		9 8		9 8		9 8
				7 6		7 6		7 6
5 4		3 4		4 —		5 4		3 4
8		8				8		o

Die o bedeutet hier, daß man nichts mehr zu suchen, sondern nur die angezeigten Inter-
valle zu nehmen habe.

*Example 4. Dissonant inflections of a 6/4 chord from Johann Philipp
Kirnberger,* Grundsätze des Generalbasses, *Berlin, 1781, p. 70.*

Although he did not credit Rameau with this insight (and indeed, he was publically a resolute critic of the Frenchman's ideas), Kirnberger was actually one of the most faithful advocates of Rameau's ideas in the later 18th century, or at least of his practical music theory. In Example 4, from Kirnberger's *Grundsätze des Generalbasses* of 1781, we can see how this idea works in the several examples given to illustrate a 6/4 chord elaborated by a number of "accidental" (*zufällige*) dissonances creating various kinds of suspensions and appoggiaturas. Other examples from the same chapter show similar accidental dissonances applied to 5/3 and 6/3 triads. The point being that the student learns that virtually all figures in the thoroughbass may be derived through *some* kind of manipulation of a triad or seventh chord, be it an inversion or some alteration of its constituent tones.

"New-fashioned Table of Signatures" (*Neumodisches Signatur-Register*)

9 9 9 9 9	9 9 9 9	9 9 9	9 9
4 5 6 7 8	5 6 7 8	6 7 8	7 8
3 4 5 6 7	3 4 5 6	3 4 5	3 4

4 5 6 7 8	5 6 7 8	6 7 8	7 8
3 4 5 6 7	3 4 5 6	3 4 5	3 4
2 2 2 2 2	2 2 2 2	2 2 2	2 2

5 6 7 8	6 7 8	7 8	8
4 5 6 7	4 5 6	4 5	4
3 3 3 3	3 3 3	3 3	3

6 7 8	7 8 8
5 6 7	5 5 6
4 4 4	4 4 4

7 8 8
6 6 7
5 5 5

Example 5. The "New-fashioned Table of Signatures" from Christoph Gottlieb Schröter, Deutliche Anweisung zum General-Bass, *Halberstadt 1772; cited in F. T. Arnold,* The Art of Accompaniment from a Thoroughbass as practised in the XVIIth and XVIIIth Centuries, *Oxford 1931 (reprint New York 1965), p. 305.*

The understanding that all harmonies could be traced back to either a triad or the seventh chord finally inspired one German thoroughbass pedagogue, Christoph Gottlieb Schröter, to apply permutation theory when calculating and ordering his figured-bass signatures. In his "New-fashioned Table of Signatures" (*Neumodisches Signatur-Register*), Schröter shows how it is possible to rotate successively the top three voices in a four-voiced structure and come up with every possible four-note combination in a diatonic context (even if some of those combinations had less than practical value). While strictly theoretical in conception, Schröter's table takes another step in using music theory to rationalize and coordinate the pedagogy of thoroughbass.

2.

CADENTIAL MOTION, THE FUNDAMENTAL BASS, AND THE RULE OF THE OCTAVE

The examples above have dealt mainly with the understanding of chordal origins and identity as encoded in figured-bass signatures. Playing the through bass, however, also entails connecting those chords. To this end, thoroughbass manuals typically would provide several paradigmatic chord progressions for the student to practice and memorize, usually with examples of correct voice-leading. In this way, the student would begin to learn the vernacular syntax of tonal music. But the question of harmonic succession naturally raises deeper theoretical questions that attracted the attention of musicians such as Rameau. The famous solution Rameau formulated to answer this problem — the *basse fondamentale*—can also be seen as originating with the practice of the thoroughbass.

While the details of Rameaus theory of the fundamental bass can become complex and vexing in their inconsistencies, his basic argument can be summarized roughly as follows: All harmony in music can be reduced to two basic categories of chords, consonant chords originating in the harmonic triad, and dissonant chords originating in the seventh chord. Each of these chords is generated from a common fundamental chord root (*son fondamental*), and this chord root remains the same regardless of the chord's inversion (as discussed above). Tonal motion is determined by the succession of these chord roots or *sons fondamentaux* and may be displayed visually in the *basse fondamentale* as a fictive bass line below the *basse continue*. The harmonies of the thoroughbass were thus shown to have been generated and controlled not by the bass voice, rather, by the fundamental bass. And the primary motion of the fundamental bass consists of precisely those intervals by which the harmonic triad was composed: perfect fifths, consonant thirds, and their inversions (fourths and sixths). Rameau would refer to such paradigmatic motion as the *basse fondamentale* (but also variously as a *progression fondamentale, succession fondamentale, route fondamentale* or *marche fondamentale*). Thus the principal of chordal generation is also seen to be the principal of harmonic succession. On this basis the entire edifice of musical composition may be constructed, one that has guided musicians without their even being aware of it:

> ... cette basse fondamentale, l'unique Boussole de l'Oreille, ce guide invisible du Musicien, qui l'a toujours conduit dans toutes ses productions, sans qu'il s'en soit encore apperçû. ... Le grand noeud de la Composition, soit pour l'Harmonie, soit pour la Melodie, consiste principalement et sur tout pour le present, dans la Basse, que nous appellons Fondamentale, et qui doit proceder en ce cas, par des Intervales consonans, qui sont ceux de la Tierce, de la Quarte, de la Quinte, et de la Sixte (*Génération harmonique*, Paris 1737, iijr, 185).

The value of the fundamental bass in Rameau's theory was both descriptive and prescriptive; it was a means of analyzing any harmonic progression and showing how it could be explained as obeying a coherent set of harmonic laws drawn from a single principle, an explanation that was in accord with the Enlightenment predilection for empirical analysis and synthesis in the sciences. At the same time, the fundamental bass offered a unique pedagogical tool for instructing beginning students in composition and accompaniment, as was made clear in the preface to a manuscript written by Rameau in the mid 1740s with the title *L'art de la basse fondamentale*:

> Apres avoir declaré ma decouverte du principe de l'harmonie et de toutes nos facultés en musique dans un seul son, apres en avoir frayé les routes dans

ce que j'appelle la basse fondle; apres en avoir exposé le rapport avec une infinité d'experiences, Traité de l'harmonie, nouveau sisteme, generation harmonique ... j'ay enfin entrepris d'en tirer une methode pour la composition et l'accompagnement sous le titre de l'art de la Basse Fondle.[13]

The major point I wish to emphasize here, however, is that the fundamental bass of Rameau was conceived through the continuo bass line, and indeed, it was written to look precisely like it was a figured bass: a linear progression of figured bass notes placed under the music that controls (here in an abstract, generative sense) the succession of acoustical harmonies heard above it.

Example 6. A "Perfect cadence" in major and minor modes from Jean-Philippe Rameau, Traité de l'harmonie, *Paris 1722, p. 57.*

---

13. F-Pi, ms 2474, fol. 1r; later heavily revised and published as Pietro Gianotti, *Le guide du compositeur,* Paris 1757. For information on this manuscript and its relation to Gianotti's gloss, see Christensen, *Rameau and Musical Thought*, pp. 309 ff.

Now let us look at a few details of the fundamental bass and see specific evidence of its filiations with the thoroughbass. In Book 2 of his *Traité*, Rameau deals exclusively with the question of chordal succession. (The first chapter of Book 2 is in fact entitled *Du son fondamental de l'harmonie, & de sa progression*.) It is not surprising that Rameau turns his attention first to the quintessential paradigm of harmonic motion, the perfect cadence. After all, this is one of the very first elementary progressions that a student is usually taught in almost every thoroughbass manual.

Rameau begins where he left off in Book 1, by noting that each of the chords in a perfect cadence (*cadence parfaite*) can be generated from their own *son fondamental*. He models the succession of these chord roots underneath the cadence (in both major and minor modes) and designates this succession — as we have seen — the *basse fondamentale*, or the fundamental bass.

Rameau then observes that the interval connecting these chord roots is a perfect fifth, which was also the primary structural interval by which the perfect triad (major and minor) was built. Through analysis of additional cadential models such as the "irregular" (plagal) cadence, as well as paradigmatic progressions such as the circle of fifths, Rameau concluded that fundamental bass motion of the fifth was the most natural of any progression. Less commonly, chords might connect by major or minor thirds, and very occasionally by ascending seconds.[14] But nature seemed to grant to the fifth priority of root motion in most tonal music. We can see how the priority of fifth motion works by looking at Rameau's analysis of probably the most ubiquitous chord progression found in just about every thoroughbass manual in the 18th century, the so-called *règle de l'octave*, or Rule of the Octave.

Now the Rule of the Octave was the standard scale harmonization students would learn to play on the keyboard (although actually, it originated in manuals of strummed instruments such as the five-

---

14. This last observation led Rameau to the startling conclusion that the same principle by which chords were generated out of fifths and thirds was the same principle that governed the succession of these chords. This remarkable synthesis in which both the construction as well as connection of chords in tonal music could be generated by the same principle became one of the bedrocks of Rameau's musical epistemology.

course guitar or theorbo—both common instruments in early continuo bands).[15] One learned the "Rule" not only as a guide for realizing an unfigured bass, but also to inculcate a feel of tonal progression by which one could improvise (or "modulate") within a given key. It is not surprising that we find the rule as a starting point in many of the *partimenti* exercises discussed elsewhere in this volume.

Example 7. "Rule of the Octave" from François Campion, Traité d'accompagnement et de composition, selon la règle des octaves de musique, *Paris 1716, p. 44.*

When Rameau wrote his *Traité* in 1722, the *Règle de l'octave* was already well established in France as a pedagogical model thanks to the advocacy of François Campion.[16] It was also implicitly, a paradigm of a "mode" for these students, in that it provided a normative harmonization of chords one would play above each scale degree of a given mode. If Rameau's theory of the fundamental bass had any legitimacy as both a theoretical model of mode, as well as a practical tool for the pedagogy of the thoroughbass, he had to show how the Rule of the Octave could be subsumed within the strictures of the fundamental bass. And this meant showing how the root of each chord in the rule largely moved by fifth motion. Example 8 shows how Rameau accomplished this in Book 4 of his *Traité.*

---

15. I have written at greater length on the history and theory of the Rule of the Octave. See Thomas Christensen, "The *règle de l'octave* in thoroughbass theory and practice," in: *Acta musicologica* 64/2 (1992), pp. 91–117.
16. François Campion, *Traité d'Accompagnement et de composition selon la règle des octaves de musique*, Paris 1716.

Example 8. "Rule of the Octave" analyzed with its fundamental bass from Jean-Philippe Rameau, Traité de l'harmonie, *Paris 1722, p. 382.*

25

The top three staves of this example show the three typical hand positions that are often illustrated in thoroughbass manuals, while the fourth staff in the bass clef shows the figures typically given the "rule". (It essentially follows Campion's harmonization given in Example 6, with two exceptions; for some reason, Rameau prolongs the first cadence in m. 7 by moving to a root-position dominant in m. 8, and he extends the final cadence at m. 17 with a flourish through an elaborated repetition of the authentic cadence.) The bottom staff indicates the fundamental bass analysis of this progression. We see that by and large, each chord was indeed connected by a fifth in the fundamental bass (or what is the same thing by inversion, a perfect fourth). A few exceptions are apparent, though. In m. 4, the movement from scale degree four to scale degree five contains an interpolated note in the fundamental bass. This D is "understood" (*sous-entendue*) according to Rameau even if not acoustically present, in order to soften the otherwise ascending second in the fundamental bass (from F to G). A similar interpolated bass is found in m. 17.

While one might object to the interpolated note as empirically unsubstantiated, this does not overshadow the greater point which is that the fundamental bass in this progression does indeed move primarily by fifth motion.[17] Rameau was convinced that by understanding mode as made up of only a few basic chords (built upon scale degrees 1, 5, 4, and 2), and each connected by fifth motion, he had made the understanding and practice of thoroughbass immensely easier. In other words, what value the Rule of the Octave possessed as a tool for learning to play the through bass was due to the *basse fondamentale* from which it was generated. Pedagogically, then, it made much more sense to begin by teaching the student the fundamental bass rather than with the Rule of the Octave. Through the latter way, he could not resist pointing out, the student was bound to learn in theory some 1584 [!] differing chords, given that a new chord would have to be mastered for every scale degree ascending and descending in every mode built upon any of the 12

17. There are also good historical as well as cognitive justifications for Rameau's employment of an interpolated note in the fundamental bass. See David Cohen, "The "Gift of Nature": Musical "Instinct" and Musical Cognition in Rameau", in: Suzannah Clark & Alexander Rehding (eds.), *Music Theory and natural Order*, Cambridge 2001, pp. 68–92.

chromatic steps, and in three or four differing hand positions. Even then, there are exceptions and limitations to the Rule:

> Le detail de ces exceptions est prodigieux; la connoissance & la pratique en sont remplies de difficultés presque insurmontables, par la multiplicité des accords, par la variation infinie de leurs Accompagnemens, par la surprise où jettent sans cesse les differentes formes de succession dont chaque accord en particulier est susceptible, & qui sont souvent contraires aux habitudes déja formées, par la confusion des regles fondamentales avec celles de gout, par le vuide que l'harmonie y souffre le plus souvent, par le peu de ressource que l'oreille y trouve pour se former aux veritables progrés des sons, par l'assujetissement trop servile aux chifres souvent fautifs, enfin par les fausses applications auxquelles des regles de détail & des exceptions innombrables ne peuvent manquer d'être sujettes.[18]

In contrast, the theory of the fundamental bass requires the student to learn only two basic chord structures — the triad and the seventh chord — and where to apply these above a given scale degree.

It ought to be pointed out that another theoretical issue was lurking in the background of this polemic: that of the priority of harmony and melody. This was to become a major issue between Rameau and Rousseau in the 1750s. But already in the 1720s, Rameau was adamant that harmony proceeds melody, the later being necessarily derivative and secondary to harmonic forces. It was not just a question of pedagogical efficacy, then. If Rameau wanted to maintain the priority of harmony, he had to show how the Rule of the Octave (which offers a harmonization of the most basic and primitive melody of all, the scale) was itself subordinate to — and generated from — the fundamental bass. It is no surprise, then, that Rameau would return again and again to this question in his subsequent theoretical writings.

The nagging problem for Rameau was not so much the irritating interpolated note he had to insert in Example 8, rather that no

---

18. "Observations sur la méthode d'accompagnement pour le clavecin qui est en usage, & qu'on appelle Echelle ou Régle de l'Octave", in: *Mercure de France* (February 1730), pp. 253–54. This quotation, incidentally, originates in a polemic Rameau had with a rival theorist and composer named Michel Pignolet de Montéclair, who took the position of advocate of the Rule of the Octave. I have discussed their quarrel in *Rameau and Musical Thought*, pp. 56–58.

harmonization seemed possible of the scale that strictly followed motion by the perfect fifth in the fundamental bass. (The nub always turned out to be between scale-degrees 6 and 7.) In his subsequent theoretical publications — the *Génération harmonique* of 1737 and the *Démonstration du principe de l'harmonie* of 1750 — he tackled anew this problem, coming up with a myriad of clever attempts to resolve the problem, although never to his satisfaction. (For one example, see below Example 9 and the attendant discussion.) Even more vexing turned out to be the harmonization of the minor scale, which offered other — and even more intractable — difficulties.[19] Still, his efforts were not all in vain. For in the course of closely analyzing the succession of harmonies that normally accompany the *Règle*, Rameau attained a number of sensitive insights in questions of harmonic *liaison* and mode, insights that would bear additional theoretical fruit. Perhaps the most important of these was that of the subdominant function.

3.

HARMONIC FUNCTIONALITY

We have noted several times that Rameau believed tonal music to be formed by only two basic constructs: the consonant triad and the dissonant seventh. Of course there were varieties of each of these constructs (minor and major for triads, and a larger number of variations for seventh chords). Still, at the most basic ontological level, tonal music could be reduced to just two families of chord, with the major triad and the "dominant seventh" serving as paradigmatic representatives of each.

A different question arose, however, when Rameau turned his attention to the problem of mode. In order to generate the mode as we have seen in the "Rule of the Octave", Rameau found it necessary to introduce harmonies on a number of differing scale degrees, not

---

19. For a discussion — and illustrations — of Rameau's many attempts to harmonize major and minor scales using only fundamental-bass motion of the fifth, see Christensen, *Rameau and Musical Thought*, pp. 193-99.

to mention the use of an interpolated fundamental bass, as we have seen in Example 8. After the publication of his *Traité de l'harmonie* in 1722, Rameau clearly was dissatisfied with his analysis of the Rule of the Octave — and implicitly of his definition of mode. For he quickly returned to this question in all of his subsequent major publications.

What had changed in Rameau's thinking was a new priority and emphasis granted to the fourth scale degree, or what he christened as the *sous-dominante*. As the name suggests, the Subdominant was considered to be the reciprocal dominant *downwards* from the tonic. Like the regular dominant, it was a perfect fifth from the tonic and participated in a cadential close on the tonic (in this case, the "irregular" or "imperfect" cadence). And also like the dominant, it too possessed a characteristic dissonance, in this case, the "added sixth." While apparently different from the seventh which would be found above the regular dominant, the added-sixth of the subdominant chord was actually generated in a similar fashion. According to Rameau, both chords have the same minor third added to their triads from opposing directions. This can be best understood through an illustration. In Example 9, we see how the F above the G triad is mirrored by the D placed *below* the F triad. In practice, though, the D normally sounds above the F triad. Both chords constitute the upper and lower dominants of C major, respectively, and both dissonances "resolve" by opposite directions to the same major third of the tonic triad. There is thus a fully symmetrical relation between the two chords that suggests the subdominant to have an ontological status on par with that of the dominant seventh.

Example 9. Rameau's Analysis of the Reciprocal structure of the Dominant Seventh and Subdominant Chord with an Added Sixth. (Cited in Christensen, Rameau and Musical Thought, *p. 184, ex. 7.6)*

I want to emphasize that this was not merely some abstract deduction Rameau drew as a consequence of his theoretical premises. On the contrary, there was a long tradition in French thoroughbass theory for adding a sixth to the triad when ascending a perfect fifth (as in the paradigmatic plagal cadence).[20] Likewise, in thoroughbass practice, the only other scale degree which might be assigned a perfect triad other than the tonic and the dominant scale degrees was that of the fourth (scale degree).[21] Still, it is simplistic to say that it was only through astute observation of practice that we find Rameau drawing his theoretical formulations. The relation of theory and practice is much more complex in Rameau's system — as it is for any sophisticated music-theoretical system. We might better say that the relation is a dialectic one in which theory suggests certain formulations that might be tested in musical practice, and conversely, musical practice suggests certain empirical data that demand explanation. The subdominant did not jump out at Rameau simply through its empirical reiteration in musical practice; it was clearly something that had a more speculative origin through his notion of the geometric progression. But if it were not for the empirical confirmation of the subdominant's prevalence in musical practice, Rameau clearly would not have developed this idea further.

Now there is much more one could say about the theoretical issues raised by Rameau's invocation of the subdominant function. (Not the least of which was the seeming contradiction in posed with his earlier theory of two primary harmonies.) But without going into further tedious detail, Rameau more or less settled on his new conviction that there were three primary and independent harmonies in any mode, and the added-sixth on scale degree four was no longer to be seen as but an inversion of a (minor) seventh chord, rather it was to be viewed as a legitimate and self-standing harmony.[22] As we

---

20. Michel de Saint-Lambert, *Nouveau traité de l'accompagnement du clavecin*, Paris 1707; trans. John S. Powell, *A New Treatise on Accompaniment*, Bloomington 1991, p. 106, ex. 127.

21. See Christensen, *Rameau and Musical Thought*, p. 179.

22. Consider these two quotes from Rameau: "Il n'y a que trois Sons fondamentaux, la Tonique, sa Dominante, qui est sa Quinte au-dessus, et sa Soudominante, qui est sa Quinte au-dessous, ou simplement sa Quarte... La seule Note tonique porte l'Accord parfait, ou naturel; on ajoute la Septiéme à cet Accord pour les Dominantes, et la Sixte majeure pour les Soudominantes" (*Géneration harmonique*, Paris 1737, p. 171); "Ces trois notes, la tonique, sa dominante et sa sous-dominante, sont les fondamentales, dont la seule harmonie compose elle de toutes les notes comprises dans l'étendue de l'octave de la tonique" (*Code de musique pratique*, Paris 1760, p. 29).

can see in Example 10, each scale degree of the major scale is harmonized either by a tonic, dominant, or subdominant chord, and all chords are connected by fifth motion. (Of course Rameau finds he can't connect scale degree 6 and 7 directly without creating stepwise motion in the fundamental bass, so he "solves" the problem by returning momentarily to scale-degree 5 before leaping to the leading tone!)

Example 10. *Analysis of the Major Scale from Rameau,*
Génération harmonique, *Paris 1737, plate 6.*

Still, the fact that Rameau could not satisfactorily harmonize the complete and uninterrupted scale using his three primary functions separated by perfect fifths in no way dissuaded him of the heuristic value of these three chords. For further analysis of musical practice convinced him that the chord of the *sous-dominante* was indeed one member of a triad of scale degrees that assumed functional priority in all tonal music. In all his following publications after the *Génération harmonique,* Rameau would continually uphold the subdominant as one of three fundamental harmonies in any key.

Rameau's theory of the subdominant became one of his most influential ideas, adopted by a number of theorists in Germany (and significantly, without the apparatus of the fundamental bass, from which is was largely disentangled). Already while Rameau was still very much alive, one theorist across the Rhine — Johann Friederich Daube — got the idea of constructing an entire peda-gogy of thoroughbass using only three harmonies after having perused a copy of Rameau's *Démonstration* shortly after it appeared in 1750. In his Germanicized version of Rameau's theory, Daube insisted that there were only three *Haupt-Accorden* in music: the tonic (*Grund Accord*), dominant seventh (*5ten Accord 7/5/3*), and subdominant (*4ten Accord 6/5/3*).[23] All other harmonies (*Neben-Accorden*) were derived by some means (familiar from Kirnberger and Schröter — inversions, suspensions, substitutions, added notes, etc.) from one of these three fundamental chords. Not being con-strained by Rameau's desiderata to privilege fifth motion in the fun-damental bass, Daube had no trouble at all providing the following luxuriant harmonization of the C major scale using inversions of his three primary chords.

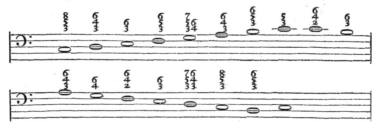

Example 11. Harmonization of the Major Scale using Three Primary Chords from Johann Daube, General-Bass in drey Accorden, Leipzig 1756, p. 20.

23. Johann Friedrich Daube, *General-Bass in drey Accorden*, Leipzig 1756. Other theorists of the time who accepted Rameau's three-chord system were William Jones, *A Treatise on the Art of Music*, London 1784, and Giordano Riccati, *Saggio sopra le leggi del contrappunto*, Trento 1762. Jones's remarks are typical: "Therefore these three keys [C, G, F] comprehend all the native harmony of the octave; and the three notes C, G, F, are the fundamental notes, because they carry all the degrees of the octave in their accompaniment" (*A Treatise on the Art of Music*, p. 13).

Now Daube himself did not theorize his pedagogy as Rameau had tried to. The three chords were simply a useful heuristic for the student learning keyboard and compositional pedagogy (much as earlier Rameau had invoked the "two-chord" system as such a heuristic). Several later generations of German theorists, however, did provide such a theoretical framework for these three harmonies, including Moritz Hauptmann, Arthur von Oettingen, and above all, Hugo Riemann, whose influential theory of harmonic functionality may be traced back to the pragmatic thoroughbass prescriptions of Rameau and Daube.[24]

4.

DIMINUTION AND PROLONGATION

One of the requirements of any competent performer of the thoroughbass was the ability to elaborate a given figured bass through stylistically-appropriate ornamentations and figures. This art of elaboration — typically called "diminution" by pedagogues of the time — was considered so fundamental to the practice of the continuo that treatises often contained dozens of pages of sample elaborations for the young student to practice and emulate. Typically, a teacher might begin with a simple bass line — perhaps a single interval, or a scale segment — and then show several dozen ways this bass line might be elaborated extemporaneously by the performer. Example 12 shows such Variation oder Veränderung of an ascending fifth provided by Friederich Niedt in his important manual of thoroughbass, the Musicalische Handleitung.

Subsequent examples by Niedt illustrate the elaboration of melodic lines and entire chordal progressions. In the latter case, he takes certain stylized dance genres — such as a sarabande — and subjects

---

24. For a concise history of functional theory in Germany, see David Bernstein, "Nineteenth-Century Harmonic Theory: The Austro-German Legacy", in: Thomas Christensen (ed.), *The Cambridge History of Western Music Theory*, Cambridge 2002, pp. 795–800; also Henry Klumpenhouwer's contribution to the same volume, "Dualist Tonal Space and Transformation in Nineteenth-Century Musical Thought", pp. 456–76.

them to a variety of diminutions and rhythmic alterations, creating in effect a suite of dance variations.[25]

Example 12. Diminutions of a Perfect Fifth from Friederich Erhardt Niedt, Musicalische Handleitung. Part 2. "Handleitung zur Variation, wie man den General-Bass und darüber gesetzte Zahlen variiren, artige Inventiones machen, und aus einem schlechten General-Bass Praeludia, Ciaconnen… leichtlich verfertigen können", Hamburg 1721; trans. Pamela Poulin & Irmgard C. Taylor, The Musical Guide, Oxford 1989, part II, p. 79.

25. On the topic of thoroughbass diminution with examples, see Joel Lester, *Composition Theory in the Eighteenth Century*, Cambridge Mass. 1992, pp. 65-68. I have also written an article on this topic that traces the history of keyboard diminution as far back as the late 15th century: Thomas Christensen, *"Fundamenta Partiturae*: Thoroughbass and Foundations of Eighteenth-Century Composition Pedagogy", in: Thomas F. Kelly & Sean Gallagher (eds.), *The Century of Bach and Mozart: Perspectives on Historiography, Composition, Theory and Practice*, Cambridge Mass. 2008, pp. 17-40.

The art of diminution was not evenly taught in all thoroughbass treatises. French manuals of the time barely mention the skill, while German writers typically offered extensive discussions of the topic with ample — and often tendentious — illustrations. The treatises of Johann David Heinichen (*Der Generalbass in der Composition*, 1728), Johann Mattheson (*Grosse General-Bass Schule*, 1731), Johann Friedrich Daube (*General-Bass in drey Accorden*, 1756), Carl Philipp Emmanuel Bach (*Versuch über die Wahre Art das Clavier zu Spielen*, 1762), and Michael Johann Wiedeburg (*Der Selbst Informirende Clavierspieler*, 1765–75) all offer copious examples of possible elaborations of continuo bass lines and chord progressions. Italian authors were inconsistent. Some, such as the London based Giorgio Antoniotto (*L'Arte Armonica or A Treatise on the Composition of Musick*, 1760) prescribed extensive exercises of harmonic elaboration for the student, while others such as Francesco Gasparini (*L'armonico pratico al cimbalo*, 1708) had little to say. (However, the practice of *partimenti*[26] undoubtedly involved the application of extensive elaborations to the bare figured bass skeleton, so we may assume that this practice was taught through oral instruction even if these instructions were never written down by the Italian maestros.) English authors were likewise inconsistent, although many did fall back into an older (seventeenth-century) tradition of melodic embellishment called "divisions" or "breaking of the ground".[27]

While this practice of continuo embellishment in all its various fashions was taught and understood as a purely practical skill, it did have "theoretical" repercussions, albeit from about two centuries later. For the practice of Baroque thoroughbass elaboration became a foundation for the music theory of the 20th-century Austrian music theorist, Heinrich Schenker. Schenker would repeatedly claim that thoroughbass embodied the structural essence of all tonal music. But not just any thoroughbass. For Schenker, it was the treatise penned by Bach's son, Carl Philip Emanuel, that provided the true light. Bach's treatise, the *Versuch über die wahre Art das Clavier zu*

---

26. Robert Gjerdingen, "*Partimenti* Written to Impart a Knowledge of Counterpoint and Composition," this volume.
27. For a discussion of this tradition, see Albert Cohen, "Performance Theory", in: Thomas Christensen (ed.), *The Cambridge History of Western Music Theory*, Cambridge 2002, pp. 540–548.

Spielen (1753–62), while never conceived by its author as a "theory" treatise, at least as understood in any 18th-century sense, was seen by Schenker as containing the seeds of the most authentic and far-reaching music theory there was. Significantly, C.P.E. Bach did not accept Rameau's theory of harmonic generation or inversion. His was largely an empirical description of practice using pure figured-bass notation. Yet in Bach's exquisitely detailed descriptions and illustrations, Schenker believed, the composer showed the greatest musical sensitivity and insight into issues of voice leading, diminution, and harmonic elaboration, elements that would of course form the essence of his own latter theory of structural hierarchy and tonal prolongation.[28] Once again, the thoroughbass provides a catalyst for profound theoretical reflection.

5.

CONCLUSION

I have tried to show in this essay how the thoroughbass in the Baroque era can be credited for stimulating some of the most searching theorizing of harmonic tonality in the 18th century — and beyond. This should really be no surprise, since the thorough-bass provided the universal notation and framework by which 18th-century musicians conceived and practiced their developing harmonic language. As it also provided pedagogical challenges for teaching this harmonic language, it makes sense that several of these thoroughbass instructors would step in and try to help clarify, sim-plify, and ultimate explain this complex empirical practice using the tools of music theory.

If not all keyboard pedagogues succumbed to this theoretical urge, for intellectually-minded musicians such as Rameau, the desire to

---

28. Schenker offers an extensive analysis of C.P.E. Bach's thoroughbass method (and particularly concerning Bach's portentous observations concerning the genre of the *Freie Fantasie*) in his essay, "The Art of Improvisation", *The Masterwork in Music, vol. 1*; trans. Richard Kramer, Cambridge 1995, esp. pp. 2–13. For more on Schenker and his theory, see William Drabkin, "Heinrich Schenker", in: Thomas Christensen (ed.), *The Cambridge History of Western Music Theory*, Cambridge 2002, pp. 812–843.

analyze and systematize thoroughbass practice within an overarching theory of harmonic tonality proved to be irresistible. For how could it be otherwise for an art that was widely equated to be commensurate with the skill of a composer?[29]

The skill of performing the thoroughbass was deemed by many pedagogues in the 18th century to be an indispensable basis for learning composition. In his widely-read treatise from 1700, Friedrich Neidt wrote one of the most famous and repeated encomiums in praise of the *General-Bass*:

> Der General-Bass ist das vollkommenste Fundament der Music welcher auf einem Clavier gespielet wird mit beyden Händen dergestalt das die lincke Hand die vorgeschriebene Noten spielet die rechte aber Con- und Dissonantien dazu greiffet damit dieses eine wolklingende Harmonie gebe zur Ehre Gottes und zulässiger Ergötzung des Gemüths.[30]

Johann Sebastian Bach, it might be noted, quoted Neidt's description in 1738 almost *verbatim* in his own compendium of General-Bass instructions cribbed from Neidt's text:

> Der General Bass ist das vollkommste Fundament der Music welcher mit beyden Händen gespielet wird dergestalt das die lincke Hand die vorgeschriebene Noten spielet die rechte aber Con- und Dissonantien darzu greift damit dieses eine wohlklingende Harmonie gebe zur Ehre Gottese und zulässiger Ergötzung des Gemüths und soll wie aller Music, also auch des General Basses Finis und End Uhrsache anders nicht als nur zu Gottes Ehre und Recreation des Gemüths seyn. Wo dieses nicht in acht genommen wird da ists keine eigentliche Music sondern in Teuflisches Geplerr und Geleyer.[31]

---

29. A good discussion illustrating the compositional potential of thoroughbass as a frame for a composer in the 18th century can be found in Joel Lester's article, "Thoroughbass as a Path to Composition in the Early Eighteenth Century", in: *Towards Tonality: Aspects of Baroque Music Theory*, Leuven 2007, pp. 145-168.
30. Friedrich Neidt, *Musicalische Handleitung*, Hamburg 1700, Ch. 2.
31. Johann Sebastian Bach, *Vorschriften und Grundsätze zum vierstimmigen spielen des General-Bass oder Accompagnement*, Leipzig 1738; cited in *Bach Dokumente II*, Kassel 1969, #433.

The designation of thoroughbass as the *fundamentum* of musical knowledge became a commonplace one in 18th-century German music theory, with varied rhetoric extolling its virtues not only as the foundation of harmony and thereby essential for the learning of musical composition, but even as a Sacred invention granted to us by God:

> ... in rechtmässigem Gebrauch/ ist und bleibt der General-Bass ein herrliche Göttliche Invention, eine solche Hauptstimm/ darinn sich all andere Stimmen/ so viel deren immer seyn mögen/ gleichsamb concentriren, und in einen Mittle-Punct zusammen ziehen... Mag demnach diese letzt-inventirte Stimm nicht unbillich Basis, compendium, Synopsis, quinta essentia &c. Das ist/ ein fundament oder Grund kurtzer Begrifff/ Auszug/ bester Safft und Krafft der gantzen Musicalischen composition gennenet werden ... [32]

> Was die rechte Anweisung zum General-Basse von Nutzen bringe lehret die Erfahrung: denn es werden erstlich die Discipul zum *Fundament* der ansgewiesen.[33]

> Das der Bassus Continuus, oder so genannte General-Bass, nechst der Composition eine von den wichtigsten und fundamentalesten Musicalischen Wissenschafften sey, dessen wird kein Music-Verständiger in Abrede seyn können.[34]

We observe in these quotations a subtle but critical shift — and conflation — of meaning from *General-Bass* as foundation of harmony to *General-Bass* as *fundament* of composition and ultimately music

---

32. Philipp Jakob Böddecker, *Manuductio nova methodico-practica ad bassum generalem*, Stuttgart 1701, p.13.
33. Andreas Werckmeister, *Harmonologia Musica*, Frankurt 1702, p.67. Cf. Werckmeister's comments in his *Die Nothwendigsten Anmerckungen und Regeln wie der Bassus Continuus oder General-Bass wol könne tractiret werden,* Aschersleben 1698: "... der General-Bass nicht anders als ein liebliches Sausen und Fundament seyn muss, in einem Musicalischen Stücke worauff das gantze Wesen beruhet... ", p.40.
34. Johann David Heinichen, *Neu erfundene und Gründliche Anweisung zu vollkommener Erlernung des General-Basses*, Leipzig 1711, p.1. Virtually identical statements may be found in Heinichen's *Der Generalbass in der Composition*, Leipzig 1728, p.1; and also David Kellner, *Treulicher Unterricht im General-Bass*, Hamburg 1732, p.1; Joseph Friederich Majer, *Neu-eröffneter theoretisch- und practischer Music-Saal*, Nürnberg 1741, p.62.

in general. In other words, fundamental as an empirical attribute of lowest voice and harmonic substratum gives way to fundamental as an ontological claim of priority and primacy as the foundation of musical composition and knowledge. The skills necessary for playing thoroughbass — how to infer and realize chords instantly above a bass line, and how to connect and embellish those chords in good taste — were exactly those required of a good composer. In short, if one could expertly play the continuo, one could also compose. And conversely, in order to compose well, one would need to understand completely the principles of the thoroughbass.

In his *Traité d'accompagnement pour le théorbe, et le clavessin*, Paris 1690, Denis Delair wrote explicitly that realizing the thoroughbass was as much an art as composition, since the "Principes de composition ... servent de fondement ä l'accompagnement." Andreas Werckmeister, in the preface to his short treatise on accompaniment emphasized the connection between mastering thoroughbass and the skill of composition, insisting that the former was the foundation of the later (a connection also made clear in the subtitle to his treatise):

> Es ist auch dieses Wercklein zugleich ein *Compendium* wie man einen *Contrapunctum simplicern componi*ren könne, denn wer einen General-Bass *absque vitiis tracti*ren will, der muss das *Fundamentum Compositionis* verstehen.[35]

Rameau, although not using the term *fondament* (which he had of course appropriated for other purposes in his theory) nonetheless held the same view:

> Les principes de composition & d'accompagnement sont les mêmes, mais dans un ordre tout-à-fait opposé. Dans la composition, la seule connoissance de la racine donne celle de toutes les branches qu'ille produit: dans l'accompagnement au contraire, toutes les branches se confondent avec leur racine.[36]

---

35. Andreas Werckmeister, *Die Nothwendigsten Anmerckungen und Regeln wie der Bassus Continuus oder General-Bass wol könne tractiret werden... Aus dem wahren Fundament der musicalischen Composition denen Anfängern zu besserer Nachricht auffgesezzet und aniezzo mercklich wermehret*, Aschersleben 1698, p. 2.
36. Jean-Philippe Rameau, *Code de musique pratique*, Paris 1760, p. 24.

The equation of composition with thoroughbass in the 18th century was clearly reflected in the titles of many of the most important treatises of the day.[37] As late as 1793, theorists such as John Casper Heck wrote that the thoroughbass "may justly be defin'd as a science form'd entirely on the fundamental principles of composition."[38] While Albrechtsberger could write "Der Generalbass ist die Fundamental-Basis der ganzen Musik. Das gründliche Studium desselben unerlässliche Bedingnis für jeden, der sich ernstlich dieses schönen Kunst weihen will."[39]

If thoroughbass remained in the estimation of most musicians a lowly, practical art,[40] there were clearly many others who saw in it something far greater: an art that at its best requires all the skills and imagination of the composer. It is not surprising, then, that many

---

37. For examples: François Campion, *Traité d'accompagnement et de composition selon la règle de l'octaves de musique*, Paris 1716; Johann David Heinichen, *Der General-Bass in der Composition*, Dresden 1728; Georg Andreas Sorge, *Vorgemach der musikalischen Composition, oder... Anweisung zum General-Bass*, Lobenstein 1745-47; Friedrich Wilhelm Marpurg, *Handbuch bey dem Generalbasse und der Composition*, Berlin 1755-60; Johann Friedrich Daube, *General-Bass in drey Accorden... dass also durch diese neue und leichte Anleitung zugleich auch zur Composition unmittelbar der Weg gebahnet wird*, Leipzig 1756; Charles-François Clement, *Essai sur l'accompagnement du clavecin,... par les principes les plus clairs et les plus simples de la composition*, Paris 1758; Johann Michael Bach, *Kurze und systematische Anleitung zum General-Bass und der Tonkunst überhaupt*, Kassel 1780; Johann Philipp Kirnberger, *Grundsätze des Generalbasses als erste Linien zur Composition*, Berlin 1781; Edward Miller, *A Treatise on Thoroughbass and Composition*, Dublin 1790.
38. John Casper Heck, *The Art of Playing the Thoroughbass*, London 1793, p. 1.
39. Ignaz von Seyfried (ed.), *Johann Georg Albrechtsberger's Sämmtliche Schriften über Generalbass, Harmonie-Lehre, und Tonsetzkunst*, Vienna 1826, p. 1.
40. For Mattheson, the thoroughbass was more *Hand-Sachen*, requiring only the keyboardist to play the harmonies designated by the chord signatures, and having a good facility of keyboard skills. But to equate this knowledge with the artistic demands of a composer (which for Mattheson above all required an instinct and understanding for natural melody) was absurd. Explaining this later point in his own manual of *General Bass* with his typical sarcasm, Mattheson said putting thoroughbass as the foundation of musical composition was like putting the cart before the horse: "Hergegen wer seinen Untergebenen sogleich über Hals und Kopf zum General-Bass führen; hernach aber, wenn er, mit saurem Schweiss ein ihm gantz unbekanntes gar nicht angenehmes Exempel, das weder gehauen noch gestochen heisst, gelernet hat, und solches daher dreschen kann, ihm erst von einer Melodie etwas vorsagen, und nach selbiger sich richten heissen vollte, (welches doch unumgänglich geschehen muss) der hätte ja wircklich die Pferde hinten den Wagen gespannet" (*Kleine General-Bass-Schule*, pp. 49-50).

of these same musicians would analyze the thoroughbass using the tools of music theory. For if the thoroughbass was indeed the *fundament* of musical composition, as so many of its champions claimed, then music theory would offer the means by which its mysteries might most clearly be brought to light—and thereby the secrets of musical composition as well.

PARTIMENTI WRITTEN TO IMPART A KNOWLEDGE OF COUNTERPOINT AND COMPOSITION

Robert Gjerdingen

Today the word "conservatory" connotes, as it has since Victorian times, an institution dedicated to conserving one of the classical performing traditions of European culture. Originally, however, a *conservatorio* was a Catholic charitable institution dedicated to conserving orphans, foundlings, and other destitute children. *I Poveri di Gesù Cristo* (The Poor Ones of Jesus Christ), the name of one of the early Neapolitan conservatories, was not just a religious metaphor. It summed up the plight and social standing of many of the students. In a world where family connections were paramount, a child without an intact family needed special assistance. If a fatherless boy could be taught a valuable skill, he might one day earn a living on his own.

1.

THE CASE OF DOMENICO CIMAROSA

Domenico Cimarosa (1749–1801) was such a boy. His father, a stonemason in Naples, had died in a fall from the aptly named palace of Capodimonte (Mountaintop). His mother survived by washing clothes at a monastery. The monks took Domenico into their school, noticed his talent for music, and arranged for him to be transferred to the *Conservatorio di Santa Maria di Loreto* at age eleven or twelve.[1] There he began eleven years of intensive training that would prepare him for gainful employment. The boy learned his lessons very well indeed, and he eventually rose to become the *maestro di capella* for empress Catherine the Great of Russia and later for emperor Joseph II of Austria.

---

1. Cimarosa was born December 17, 1749. He entered the conservatory in 1761. The exact date of his admission has not been established.

The Estense library in Modena has preserved a small book of *partimenti* — instructional basses — dated 1762 and catalogued as the earliest known work of Cimarosa.[2] The date and name are secure, given that the manuscript is clearly dated and bears several instances of the young Cimarosa's signature. But the *partimenti* that it contains were all, or nearly all,[3] composed by the great Neapolitan *maestro* Francesco Durante (1684-1755). The manuscript, rather than being a collection of original works by a precocious twelve-year-old, is in all likelihood Cimarosa's *zibaldone*,[4] which could be translated variously as "commonplace book", "notebook," or "lesson book". While dozens, perhaps hundreds, of *partimento* manuscripts have survived from the eighteenth century,[5] very few were dated or signed. Cimarosa's manuscript gives us a rare glimpse into what a famous composer, at a specific early age, was absorbing from lessons traceable to the recently deceased Durante. It also tells us what sort of lessons Cimarosa's own teachers, the *maestri* Fedele Fenaroli (1730-1818), Antonio Sacchini (1730-1786), and Gennaro Manna (1717-1779), deemed fitting for the training of a bright student.

Some of the *partimenti* in Cimarosa's lesson book were clearly designed to teach important compositional schemata like *La romanesca* and *La folia*. Example 1 shows the opening measures of the bass line and chord progression of *La romanesca*,[6] best known today perhaps through Pachelbel's *Canon in D*. The lower staff shows the *partimento* as given in the manuscript. On the upper staff I have indicated where *La romanesca* ends and the cadence begins, and I have notated the typical right-hand part that Cimarosa would have been

---

2. *The New Grove Dictionary of Music and Musicians*, 2nd ed., 2001, in its entry "Cimarosa", adopts the Estense cataloging and the attribution to Cimarosa: "Partimenti, ?vc, kbd, 1762, I-MOe."

3. While many of the exercises are exact copies of Durante's, others are abridgments or adaptations.

4. Francesco Galeazzi, in his *Elementi teorico-pratici di musica con un saggio sopra l'arte di suonare il violino analizzata, ed a dimostrabili principi ridotta, vol. 2*, Rome 1796, pp. 54-55, refers to a student musician's lesson book as a *zibaldone*.

5. Almost every major library with collections of eighteenth-century music has copies of *partimenti* by the great maestros of Naples and Bologna.

6. This bass pattern with its attendant harmonies, though frequently called *La romanesca* in the period from the later sixteenth through the seventeenth century, was also given different names at different times and places. No claim is made that the Neapolitans used this name for this pattern, though there is also no evidence that any other name was used.

expected to play. The figured bass for the cadence is in the hand of the original scribe. The many "5"s, which were self-evident to adults who knew that this bass required each chord to be in root position, are shown in parentheses to indicate that they are by a different scribe and may have been added by Cimarosa himself or a later hand.

Example 1. Bass staff: the Romanesca *pattern and cadence as found in Cimarosa's student notebook. Treble staff: a modern realization of this* partimento. *The figures for the cadence appear to be original. The figures for the* Romanesca *appear to have been added later (the parentheses are a modern addition to indicate the different hand).*

Example 2. Bass staff: the Folia *pattern as found in Cimarosa's student notebook. Treble staff: a modern realization of this* partimento. *The figures shown in parentheses appear to have been added later.*

Example 2 shows the opening measures of Durante's *partimento* of *La folia*, a traditional pattern that served as the theme of twenty-four caprices for violin by Corelli, which in turn inspired many later variations like those by Liszt and Rachmaninoff. Again, the lower staff presents the *partimento*, and the upper staff presents a likely realization. The markings of "5/3" chords, again self-evident to an adult musician, were probably added by a student or a later hand. As these examples demonstrate, such traditional compositional schemata were directly taught to students through *partimenti*. The complete pattern was not, however, written down. The student had to internalize the pattern and had to be able to play the full pattern from the sole cue of the bass.

The example of *La folia* is found on the verso of the ninth folio in this manuscript. The recto side contains a longer *partimento* in 12/8 time and the key of A minor. In the process of learning Durante's A-minor *partimento*, a talented boy like Cimarosa would surely have noticed an incongruity when a busy, interesting opening passage leads into a boring passage of isolated, almost static tones (Ex. 3).

Example 3. The opening measures of an A-minor partimento *from Cimarosa's student notebook. The first two measures, with their active eighth notes in 12/8 time, lead first to a cadence and then to a passage (mm. 4-5) with hardly any melodic interest.*

Note that the redundant figures for the "boring" passage, "8" and "3", do not add any information about harmony, since the intervals they represent are always assumed to be present in the absence of specific figures to the contrary. Instead, the redundant figures are meant to give clues to the position of an upper voice. Could the "interesting/foreground" passage transposed an octave higher (= "8") combine with the "boring/background" passage to form a proper two-voice counterpoint? The answer is a definitive "yes," as shown in Example 4.

Example 4. With regard to the partimento *shown in Ex. 3, its "boring" passage of mm. 4-5 can serve as a contrapuntal accompaniment to the "interesting" passage of mm. 1-2.*

Example 5. A G-minor partimento *from Cimarosa's notebook. Like the* partimento *in Ex. 3, this* partimento *begins with an "interesting" passage that, following a cadence, leads to a "boring" passage.*

On the verso side of *La Romanesca*, Cimarosa would encounter another Durante bass (Ex. 5), which is so similar to the one shown in Example 4 as to suggest that both share the same compositional schema—an opening 1–2–3 pattern extended to the fourth scale degree, or fa, and then followed by a cadence. As in Example 4, the bass in Example 5 features an "interesting/foreground" and a subsequent "boring/background". And as one might now begin to expect, the foreground and background combine in proper two-voice counterpoint, as shown in Example 6.

Example 6. With regard to the partimento *shown in Ex. 5, its "boring" passage of mm. 3-5 can serve as a contrapuntal accompaniment to the "interesting" passage of mm. 1-2.*

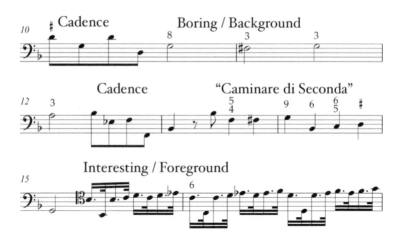

Example 7. A more elaborate G-minor partimento *from Cimarosa's notebook. Like the* partimenti *in Exx. 3 and 5, this* partimento *begins with an "interesting" passage (not shown) that, following a cadence, leads to a "boring" passage. Following a sequence of 2–3 suspensions (caminare di seconda), the "interesting" passage of the previous G-minor section is restated in B-flat major.*

Example 8. With regard to the partimento *shown in Ex. 7, its "boring" passage of mm. 10-12 can serve as a contrapuntal accompaniment to the "interesting" passage (e.g., Ex. 8, mm. 8-9, mm. 15-16, or m. 18).*

Whether Cimarosa was told which passages of a *partimento* to combine, or whether he was expected to intuit the correct combination by himself, one can easily infer that sooner or later the game of combining passages in Durante *partimenti* would become well learned. On the page facing the *partimento* of Example 3, Cimarosa would have studied the passage shown in Example 7. There he would encounter an "interesting/foreground" passage followed by a cadence. Then he would find a passage of the same length but clearly "boring/background". After a second cadence there comes a chain of 2–3 suspensions in the implied upper voices (one can infer the series from the figured bass and context). Other, similar sequences in Cimarosa's notebook were called *caminare di...* ("traveling or progressing by", in this case, seconds and thirds). Again, it is difficult to imagine a musician with Cimarosa's talent failing to recognize the same game of a contrapuntal *ars combinatoria*. Example 8 shows the "winning" combination.

It was through the experience of playing *partimenti* that this author first noticed the contrapuntal implications of the types of opening passages in Cimarosa's notebook. When the "interesting" part ceased, one naturally wondered what ought to happen next. With the sound of the interesting, thematic part still in one's memory, it was only a small step to connect that memory with the "boring" accompaniment. Many other authors, in discussing *partimenti*, have made general comments on the motivic and contrapuntal play implicit in them, and counterpoint is so obvious in the fugal *partimenti* as to require no special mention. But to my knowledge Tharald Borgir, in his dissertation of 1971, later adapted for his 1987 book *The Performance of the Basso Continuo in Italian Baroque Music*,[7] was the first modern author to point to specific opening passages in Durante *partimenti* that suggest contrapuntal combinations. His examples were taken from Durante's *partimenti diminuiti*, while Cimarosa's notebook contains selections from Durante's *regole* and *partimenti numerati*, but the practice is similar in all these collections. Indeed, the practice seems to have been widespread among most of the Neapolitan maestros.

---

7. Tharald Borgir, *The Performance of the Basso Continuo in Italian Baroque Music*, Ann Arbor 1987.

2.
SELECTED *PARTIMENTI* OF
NICCOLO ZINGARELLI

In his final years at the conservatory, Cimarosa was advanced to the chapel-master class of future composers, where his classmates were Giuseppe Giordani (1751-1798) and Niccolò Zingarelli (1752-1837). Zingarelli would go on to hold some of the most important positions in eighteenth-century Italy, including *maestro di capella* at the cathedrals of Naples and Milan, music director of St. Peter's in Rome, and, in the early nineteenth century, director of the combined conservatories of Naples. He carried on the Durante tradition of composing a number of *partimenti* that call for the contrapuntal combination of different passages. In Example 9, taken from an early nineteenth-century print of more than a hundred of his *partimenti*,[8] two measures of active eighth notes are followed by two measures of long tones marked *imit* (an abbreviation of *imitazione,* making explicit what was implicit in earlier collections).

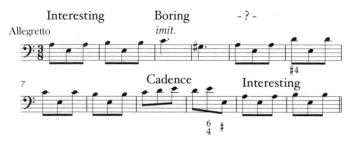

Example 9. A simple A-minor partimento *by Zingarelli. Its first two measures are active, while mm. 3-4 are relatively static.*

While it is fairly obvious that the opening, "interesting" eighth notes, which outline a type of Do–Re–Mi ascent, might be played in a soprano voice over the long, "boring" tones in the bass, it is visually unclear what follows. As it turns out, the two voices can continue in

---

8. Nicolò Zingarelli, *Partimenti del signor maestro Don Nicolò Zingarelli...* , Milan [ca. 1820s].

canon until the first cadence (see Ex. 10), after which the imitation begins again. For the cadence, the student could draw upon memories of any standard close, and the cadence shown in Example 10 is merely one suggestion.

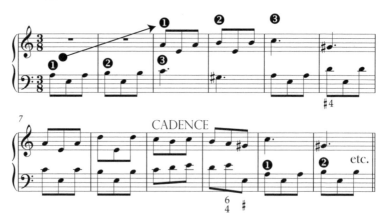

Example 10. With regard to the partimento *shown in Ex. 9, its "boring" passage of mm. 3-4 can serve as a contrapuntal accompaniment to the "interesting" passage of mm. 1-2. In addition, the treble voice can continue in canon with the bass until the cadence of mm. 9-10. Then, in m. 11, the same canon begins again.*

In Example 11, we encounter another instance of Zingarelli's pervasive use of this type of counterpoint. Because I suspect the reader has by now become adept at guessing the combinations, only the final result is shown, where the lower staff presents the original *partimento* and the upper staff presents a reconstruction of the added part. As the example demonstrates, the combination of the "interesting" 1–2–3 rising melody against the "boring" long tones recurs over and over in these opening measures of the *partimento*. In measure 6, the expected melodic "E" fails to occur in the *partimento*, but emerges in the added part to fit the indicated figures perfectly. That melody can continue to rise, merging in measure 7 with the 1–2–3 theme now in F major.

In Example 12, Zingarelli presents a theme whose regular alternation of tonic and dominant harmonies allows for *three*-voice counterpoint, with a new entry of the flowing eighth notes occurring every two measures. To highlight the counterpoint, I show the example with two reconstructed upper parts, even though both could be played by a single hand. Note that a student needed to be constantly aware of the key and of upcoming modulations. In measure 18, for instance, the *partimento* moves toward the key of F minor, which requires a slight alteration (at the asterisk) in the melody. Once F minor is firmly established, the three-part counterpoint can begin again in the new key. There is a skilled pedagogy at work in such an exercise. Notice, for instance, how when the theme returns in measure 11, it rises and falls as before. But in place of the simple quarter note that previously concluded its descent, Zingarelli now presents a tied quarter note (mm. 13-14). He introduces a suspension in place of the simpler original theme. The student thus learns how the suspension works in context, without needing to be told the details of counterpoint. Moreover, the student absorbs the sense of a suspension as a decoration or ornament of the basic theme.

Example 11. Bass staff: a D-minor partimento by Zingarelli. Treble staff: a modern demonstration first of how the "interesting" opening passage of the bass can serve as the melody in mm. 3-4, and second of how that passage fits well in each of the remaining measures.

Example 12. Bass staff: a C-minor partimento by Zingarelli. Treble staves: a modern demonstration of how the "interesting" opening passage of the bass can serve as the source material for three-part counterpoint.

3.

THE *PARTIMENTI* OF GIOVANNI PAISIELLO

Cimarosa and Zingarelli learned the *partimenti* of Durante from
students of Durante. Giovanni Paisiello (1740-1816) had the opportunity to study with Durante himself during the maestro's final
year (1755). Paisiello, following his training in Naples, embarked
on a highly successful career as an opera composer. His rising fame
was noticed at the Russian court in St. Petersburg, and in consequence he was recruited into the service of Catherine the Great
(1729-1796). He arrived in St. Petersburg in 1776 and remained
until 1783 (Cimarosa would follow him later, serving from 1787 to
1791). Paisiello's sojourn in Russia is perhaps best remembered for
the production of his *Il barbiere di Siviglia* ("The Barber of Seville",
September 1782), whose character Figaro, from the French plays of
Beaumarchais, would reappear to great effect in Mozart's *Le nozze
di Figaro* (May 1786) and Rossini's *Il barbiere di Siviglia* (February
1816). But that same year Paisiello also published a book of *partimenti* (1782)[9] for his student and patroness the grand duchess Maria
Fyoderovna (1759-1828). While that name certainly looks Russian,
she, like Catherine the Great, was born in the Prussian city of Stettin.
To her second Christian name, Marie, was added the Russian pat-
ronymic "Fyoderovna", meaning "daughter of Friedrich". She was
brought to Russia to marry Catherine's son Paul and subsequently
became the Tsarina upon Catherine's death (1796). Thus the very
high status of this "Grand Duchess of All the Russias" (as she was
described on the title page of Paisiello's *partimenti*) may in some
way account for the unprecedented act of printing these exercises.
Up to that time, *partimenti* had been known only through manuscript copies, even the universally lauded *partimenti* of Durante. The
partimento Regole (Rules) of Fenaroli had been printed in Naples
in 1775,[10] but that edition included only the rules themselves, with
the musical examples remaining in manuscript. To my knowledge,

9. Giovanni Paisiello, *Regole per bene accompagnare il partimento*, St. Petersburg 1782.
10. Fedele Fenaroli, *Regole musicali per i principianti di cembalo*, Naples 1775; reprint
Bologna 1975.

no Italian collection of the *partimenti* of a major maestro had been printed before Paisiello's, and none would be printed again until the *partimenti* of Cimarosa's teacher Fedele Fenaroli (1730–1818) appeared in the very early nineteenth century, both in Italy and in France.

This St. Petersburg edition of *partimenti,* all of which, according to its dedication page, were composed by Paisiello, followed the general outline of the large Neapolitan manuscript collections of Durante's *partimenti.* There were typically four sections: (1) *regole* or rules, (2) *partimenti numerati* or figured basses with simpler realizations, (3) *partimenti diminuiti* or unfigured basses with more florid realizations, and (4) *fughe* or fugues. Paisiello's print retains an obvious "rules" section, proceeds to figured basses, then to unfigured basses, and ends with a very large number of *partimenti* that contain obvious or openly marked points of imitation. Let us examine each section in turn.

3.1 RULES

The "rules" or *regole* of a *partimento* treatise are typically presented in the form of short definitions or exhortations. For example, Paisiello defines a pedal point as follows:

> Una nota tenuta di piu battute ... [con] varij accordi ... vien chiamata pedale.[11]

Each such rule, or set of related rules, is exemplified by a small *partimento.* In the case of the pedal point, he provides the *partimento* shown in Example 13 (from Paisiello's p. 13). Perhaps because these simplest exercises presume an audience of beginners, the figures are given predominantly in a "literal" form with the vertical stack of numbers arranged like the stack of tones in the chords. That is, the top number represents the top or soprano tone, and the lower numbers represent lower tones.

---

11. *A (bass) note held for several beats... with changing chords... is called a "pedal."* from Giovanni Paisiello, *Regole per bene accompagnare il partimento,* St. Petersburg 1782, p. 13.

Example 13. A G-major partimento *by Paisiello. This is an exercise for beginners in figured bass. The student is given more figures than an expert would require. For instance, the first chord in m. 1—3/5/8—would normally receive no figures at all, since a simple triad was the default expectation.*

Example 14. A modern realization in a simple chordal style of Paisiello's partimento *from Ex. 13. The annotations above the treble staff indicate how this small* partimento, *while quite simple, nevertheless incorporates many of the important formal milestones of much larger pieces.*

The *partimento* of Example 13 gives opportunities for the student to attempt (in general terms) an opening presentation of a theme or subject, a modulation, a varied restatement of the theme in the new key, a digression, a sequence, an approach to the pedal point, the pedal point, and a succession of increasingly stronger cadences — skills that would later apply directly to composing a sonata, aria, or motet. These contexts are marked on Example 14, which is this author's simple chordal realization of Paisiello's figured bass. This realization follows in the main the literal figures of Example 13, but departs from them when necessary to create smoother lines in the upper parts.

3.2 FIGURED BASSES

As the discussion passes from intervals to modulations, Paisiello introduces longer *partimenti* with complete figuring. For example, he notes how a raised forth or a lowered second can lead to a modulation:

> La Quarte Maggiore hà la forza di far variare il Tono, cosi ancora è necessario sapere, che la Seconda Minore hà l'istessa forza, ... [12]

Example 15. A G-minor partimento by Paisiello. This more advanced figured bass uses over-specific figures, such as the opening 5/3/8, to indicate voicings. For instance, the suggested "5" in the soprano at the first chord connects with the "7–6–5" descent indicated in the second half of m. 1. That descending pattern become a recurring motive in this partimento.

In these more advanced exercises the figures are now mostly in normal form with the highest number being placed highest regardless of

---

12. *The raised fourth [scale degree] has the power to alter the key, and it should be noted that the lowered second [scale degree] has the same power,...* from Giovanni Paisiello, *Regole per bene accompagnare il partimento*, St. Petersburg 1782, p. 21.

the particular voicing of the chords. Yet occasionally the numbers do indicate particular movements in the upper parts. In Example 15 (from Paisiello's p. 21), notice the emphasis on a four-tone descending motif (required by the figures "7 6 5 3") that later returns preceded by three iterated eighth notes (cf. the "8 8 8" in mm. 9 and 12).

Such *partimenti* look similar to ordinary figured-bass accompaniments. Yet the goal seems to have been broader: the inculcation of motivic and consequently contrapuntal thinking. As shown in this author's realization of Example 16, the motivic interplay between melody and bass can become a pervasive feature of this *partimento.*

Example 16. A modern realization, with two upper parts, of Paisiello's partimento *from Ex. 15.*

3.3 UNFIGURED BASSES

Paisiello begins his section of unfigured basses with small, plain exercises. But they are not simple to realize, given the many modulations. Learning to recognize the "affordances" of this bass — the set of accompaniment patterns that will match the shape of the bass — can help to simplify the task of interpreting this type of bass. The bass of Example 17 (from p. 23), for instance, may at first glance look like a wandering series of quarter notes and half notes, yet to the Neapolitan student it contained a clear chain of signals or cues to a set of stock patterns.

Example 17. An unfigured C-major partimento *by Paisiello. For students in Naples, figures were somewhat like training wheels on bicycles. Once one could get "up and running" with the figures, one moved on to unfigured basses. A student needed to know how to re-create a number of small contrapuntal-harmonic schemata for any typical passage in such a bass.*

I have described in detail a set of stock patterns known to Neapolitan students in the monograph *Music in the Galant Style*.[13] Example 18 presents a sample realization of Example 17 with annotations of the schemata described in that book. The Jupiter is a typical opening gambit, named after the opening of the last movement of Mozart's "Jupiter" symphony. The Prinner, named after a seventeenth-century theorist, is the common riposte to an opening theme. Here the Jupiter-Prinner pair constitutes, in sonata terminology, the first theme, and it recurs in measures 4-7 as the second theme (in G major initially). Were this *partimento* a small sonata, the double bar would occur at the rests in measure 12. Like early sonatas, the first theme begins the second half of the movement, only in the key of the dominant (G major). The major-then-minor pattern named a Fonte[14] by Riepel in 1755 (Italian for a well or spring; here a Prinner in D minor followed by one in C major) brings the tonality back to C major for the presentation of the final cadences. So although the

13. Robert O. Gjerdingen, *Music in the Galant Style: Being a Treatise on Various Schemata Characteristic of Eighteenth-Century Music for Courtly Chambers, Chapels, and Theaters, Including Tasteful Passages of Music Drawn from Most Excellent Chapel Masters in the Employ of Noble and Noteworthy Personages, Said Music All Collected for the Reader's Delectation on the World Wide Web*, New York 2007.
14. Joseph Riepel, *Anfangsgründe zur musicalischen Setzkunst: Nicht zwar nach alt-mathematischer Einbildungs-Art der Zirkel-Harmonisten sondern durchgehends mit sichtbaren Exempeln abgefasset, ii: Grundregeln zur Tonordnung insgemein*, Frankfurt and Leipzig 1755.

bass of Example 17 looks quite simple on paper, it was intended as a microcosm of galant compositional technique, combining melody, harmony, counterpoint, and form.

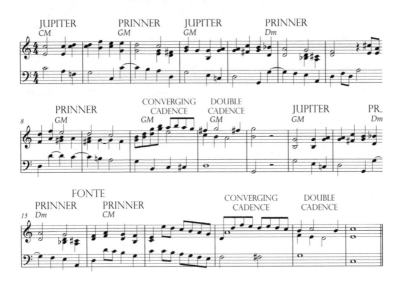

Example 18. A modern realization, with two (or occasionally three) upper parts, of Paisiello's partimento *from Ex. 17. The annotation above the treble staff indicates various phrase and cadential schemata characteristic of the galant style.*

Only five pages later (p. 28) the level of difficulty rises dramatically. One wonders how many courtiers in St. Petersburg could have managed to perform Example 19, an excerpt demanding a florid treatment in concerto style? The passage shown begins at measure 15, where the figures indicate a call-and-response exchange between melody and bass. In measure 20, at the soprano clef, Paisiello writes out a two-part solo. This is typical of Neapolitan *partimenti*, where, in the terminology of the concerto, *soli* were written out and *tutti* had to be realized from just a bass. The changing of clefs to indicate the entry of a soloist or other new part becomes more common as *partimenti* become more difficult, culminating in the *partimento* fugue. There each new entry of the subject or answer tends to be introduced with the clef appropriate for its range (the alto voice takes the alto clef, etc.).

Example 19. A largely unfigured C-major partimento by Paisiello. The figures in mm. 15-18 cue a call-and-response interplay between treble and bass. In m. 20, the switch to soprano clef indicates a fully notated solo passage, as in a concerto. The figures in m. 22 alert the player to the beginning of an ascending sequence.

Based on the concerto repertory of Paisiello and Durante's time, it is clear that motives from the tutti reappear in the soli. For the listener, of course, the tutti come first, and the soli are perceived as making decorative variations on motives from the tutti. But in concerto-like *partimenti*, the performer must re-create the tutti from the clues of the soli. In other words, the performer needs first to study the whole *partimento* before essaying a realization. Example 20 gives this author's realization of Example 19.

3.4 IMITATION

Paisiello replaces the typical final, fugal section of *partimenti* with a long section devoted to *imitazione*:

> N. B. L'imitazione s'intende, quando un Canto propone qualche passaggio, e da un' altro si risponde dell' istessa maniera: come si vedrà dall' esempie ...[15]

---

15. "Note that one should understand "imitation" as occurring when one voice sets out a certain passage and then another voice responds to it in the same manner, as you will see in the examples [that follow]..." from Giovanni Paisiello, *Regole per bene accompagnare il partimento*, St. Petersburg 1782, p. 29.

Nearly 60 percent of his book is devoted to the study of *imitazione*. Like Zingarelli, he placed that word on the score wherever he wanted to draw attention to the need for an imitative exchange between melody and bass. But many more opportunities for imitation are implicit in each *partimento*.

Example 21 (from p.34) shows an elaborate *partimento* from this section on imitation. In schematic terms, an opening Romanesca (mm. 1-2) with Prinner riposte (mm. 3-4) leads into a long series of *movimenti*. *Movimenti* (It.: "moves" or "motions") were sequential bass patterns whose preferred realizations were spelled out in the *regole* of Durante. The *movimento* of measures 1-2 was cued by a bass "falling a fourth, rising a second." The *movimento* of measure 4 and following was "rising a fourth, falling a fifth". In measure 26, the *movimento* of "rising a fourth, falling a third" receives an explicit indication of *imitazione*. It seems likely that the imitative upper part will initiate its upward leaps during the rests in the lower part. The suggested imitation in measure 48 presumably calls for the quarter notes of the previous measure to accompany the whole notes of measure 48.

Example 22 presents this author's realization of the *partimento* of Example 21. It is notated as four separate voices on two staves in order to bring out the imitative interplay between the voices. Note that the *partimento* of Example 21 was, after the first three measures, largely unfigured. The initial figures were to fix the specific suspensions of the Romanesca and to cue the following Prinner. Measures 35-36 are figured so as to cue one of the stock ways of realizing an ascending scale. This figuring might not have been necessary had Paisiello not wanted to make an explicit motivic connection with measures 40-41. Though not immediately obvious, the figures of measures 40-41 result in the same upper part specified by the figures in measures 35-36, thus reinforcing the close connection between these two different *movimenti*, both of which share the function of ascending sequences. The last complete set of figures is given to the pedal point. Pedal points were often figured because the bass alone gave no clue to the desired texture. These figures are essentially the same as those for the pedal point in the earlier Example 13.

Example 20. A modern realization, with two upper parts, of Paisiello's partimento *from Ex. 19. The annotations above the treble staff indicate how this* partimento *mimics the solo and tutti passages of a concerto.*

Example 21. A large and complex D-major partimento *by Paisiello. The few figures added to the bass indicate: mm. 1-2, a series of suspensions added to the* Romanesca *bass; mm. 4-7, a chain of seventh chords in a circle-of-fifths progression; m. 24, a reminder of the local key (B min.); m. 33, a "tenor" cadence on the dominant (A maj.); mm. 35-37, a sequence to ornament the ascending scale in the bass; mm. 40-41, another sequence which can use the same motives as in mm. 35-37; m. 59, the approach to a cadenza or pedal point; and mm. 60-62, the details of a sequence above the dominant pedal point. The word* Imitazione *in m. 26 indicates a sequential imitation in the upper voice of the two-note motive in the bass. By contrast, the same word in m. 48 indicates an imitation in the upper voice of the quarter-note passage from the previous measure.*

This elaborate *partimento* helped the student to explore all manner of connections between a variety of motives in the melody and the bass. The *imitazione* required in measure 48, for instance, takes place over a descending fourth in whole notes. That is the same bass of the opening theme, meaning that the moving quarter notes of measure 47, the descending whole notes of measure 48, and the opening melody of measure 1 can all be combined in measure 50. The complete combination, shown in Example 22, is not contrapuntally flawless.

Example 22. A modern realization of Paisiello's partimento *from Ex. 21.*

But *partimenti* in the Durante tradition were meant to be performed, not transcribed and examined. The tradition encouraged combinations — the *ars combinatoria*. One can, for instance, take a version of the moving quarter notes of measure 47, combine it with the pedal point beginning in measure 60, and then add a version of the opening melody above this rich combination to create a type of climax of imitation and combination.

(example 22: continuation)

(example 22: final)

4.

CONCLUSIONS

The period from Durante's appointment as *secondo maestro* at the *Conservatorio di Sant' Onofrio a Porta Capuana* (1710), one of the four original Neapolitan conservatories, to Zingarelli's appointment as director of the consolidated *Real Collegio di Musica* (1813), which absorbed the remnants of the old conservatories, represents a century in which Neapolitan training appears to have given young composers an advantage over most of their European contemporaries, judging from the extraordinary number of important positions, commissions, and honors they received. When Charles Burney, for instance, named the four greatest composers of opera ("Jomelli, Galuppi, Piccini, and Sacchini") in 1770, three out of the four had been trained in Naples.[16] Rigorous training in *partimenti* seems to have played a role in fostering excellence in composition, and perhaps it is not entirely coincidental that people outside of Naples with connections to training in *partimenti* were also among the most famous musicians of their day (Padres Martini and Mattei in Bologna trained students like J. C. Bach, Rossini, and Donizetti; and the Bach circle in central Germany gave their students fugal *partimenti* as evidenced by the Langloz manuscript[17]). *Partimenti* may have provided models for how to adapt principles of strict counterpoint to the prevailing galant style. The many opportunities for imitative counterpoint in *partimenti* helped the student discover how real melodies could be combined in an artistic manner. In this sense *partimenti* developed a student's contrapuntal imagination through guided exploration of the *ars combinatoria* — the "art of combinations".

It has always been evident that the apex of the *partimento* tradition involved the *partimento* fugue. Fugues came last in *partimento* manuscripts, suggesting that they were the ultimate exercises prior to

16. Charles Burney, *The Present State of Music in France and Italy* (2nd ed.), London 1773.
17. William Renwick (ed.), *The Langloz Manuscript: Fugal Improvisation Through Figured Bass*, Oxford 2001.

attempts at professional-level composition. Perhaps that is why, for his amateur patroness, Paisiello did not include fugues in his publication. What has been much less evident is the degree to which the art of contrapuntal combinations and of simple patterns of imitation was already taught in the *partimenti* that a student would have learned *prior* to encountering *partimento* fugues. Fugue involves a particular type of formal, imitative counterpoint that, as the modern student may come to realize, can be almost impossibly difficult to write without a thorough background in the more general type of counterpoint taught in *partimenti*. The modern student, even if prepared by training in separate areas like harmony and species counterpoint, often lacks experience in integrating those domains. For the eighteenth-century student in Naples, by contrast, strict counterpoint, harmony through figured bass, and common types of imitation were all tightly integrated through training in *partimenti*. Composition and counterpoint became almost the same subject, a circumstance reflected in the term that eighteenth-century writers and musicians often used when referring to composers: *contrapuntisti* (contrapuntists). Though the conservatories of Naples enrolled some of the poorest, least educated boys in Italy, they graduated many of the most famous composers of that era. Today, to understand how such transformations were possible, we may need to study *partimenti* ourselves.

PARTIMENTO-FUGUE:
THE NEAPOLITAN ANGLE

Giorgio Sanguinetti

After a long period of oblivion, the *partimento* tradition seems now to have awakened the attention of the musical community. After a century-long hiatus between composition and performance, and — more generally — between theory and practice, many musicians are now fascinated by a mode of transmission of knowledge that aimed at a non-mediated, unreflected musical competence through what Robert Gjerdingen has called "ritual model of shared symbolic practices".[1] In fact, the practice of *partimento* allowed a global composition training — thoroughbass, harmony, counterpoint, form, texture, motivic coherence — through improvisation. As a reward for a long and difficult practice, the student attained the highest degree of musical knowledge: a quasi-automatic, instinctive compositional skill, a way of composing "through the fingers". A skill that, enabling a composer to write an opera in one or two weeks (if he was requested to do so), was particularly appropriate to an era with a turbulent and unstable musical market.

The direct relation between academic training and artistic production was also made possible by the fact that the school exercises the students worked on were not different from the music they would compose as professional musicians. In fact, *partimenti* were never dry exercises. Even the simplest ones were always musically conceived, and many of them still have a real artistic value. The sharp distinction between Art (inspired by the Spirit) and the exercise (mechanical and uninspired, and thus devoid of any real content), typical of the idealistic ideology, was not yet operating in eighteenth century musical culture.

The *partimento* tradition originated in Italy, and developed mainly in Naples during the eighteenth century. The four conservatories of

---

1. Robert Gjerdingen, "Partimenti in Their Historical Context", in: *Monuments of Partimenti — A Series Presenting the Great Collections of Instructional Music Intended for the Training of European Court Musicians*, http://faculty-web.at.northwestern.edu/ gjerdingen/partimenti/index.htm.

Naples — Santa Maria di Loreto (established 1537), Sant'Onofrio in Capuana (1578), Santa Maria della Pietà dei Turchini (1583) and Poveri di Gesù Cristo (1589) — have been the first professional music schools in Europe. During the eighteenth century they were regarded as depositories of an almost legendary excellence in teaching, particularly for singing and composition. The Neapolitan methods for composition teaching were based essentially on keyboard improvisation (based on *partimento*) and on strict counterpoint. Free composition came later, and was approached through short, wordless pieces for voice and basso continuo called *solfeggi*, and open-scored exercises called *disposizioni* (more on this subject later).

Of the many different genres and styles that a *partimento* can embody (for example: sonata, toccata, two-voice invention, concerto), the fugue is the most difficult one. Hence, fugues were generally recognized as the crowning glory of any serious musical education. In fact, in many *partimenti* collections ordered by increasing difficulty (like those of Durante, Cotumacci, Sala, or Fenaroli, see Table 1) the fugues appear at the end of the book. However, the Neapolitan masters used two distinct, but converging, paths to approach the fugue. One is the *partimento*-fugue; the other is the vocal fugue. The first, as the final stage of *partimento* training, was (at least in the eighteenth century) improvised; the second, as the arrival point of counterpoint study, was always written.[2]

Every composition student in the four Naples conservatories had to follow both approaches (improvised and written) to the fugue, and famous masters such as Leo, Sala and Fenaroli, wrote instructions for both. Fenaroli composed the most revered *partimento*-fugues, but also left examples of vocal fugues in a work titled *Studio di contropunto*, of which a few manuscript copies survive.[3] Fenaroli's approach to vocal fugue is close to Leo's *Istituzioni e regole di con-*

---

2. In eighteenth century Italy the term *contrappunto* was often used in a broad sense, and indicated the art of composing well-written music in whatever style (not only fugues, canons and the like); and *contrappuntista* was the title accorded to an expert composer.
3. *Studio di contropunto del Sig. D. Fedele Fenaroli*. Naples: Biblioteca del Conservatorio S. Pietro a Majella, MS 22.2.6-2. Another manuscript copy of essentially the same work (although the content is not identical) is *Studi, o sia scuola di contropunto del Sig. D. Fedele Fenaroli. Per uso di Ferdinando Sebastiani* (1819). Naples: Biblioteca del Conservatorio S. Pietro a Majella, MS 22.1.23.

trappunto, a manuscript bearing the year 1792 which is clearly a copy of an older original, perhaps now lost.[4] And, just as Fenaroli, Leo too wrote some of the finest examples of *partimento*-fugues.

Partimento and vocal fugues may be considered as complementary. The *partimento*-fugue was improvised, but with the aid of a solid, continuous thread (the *partimento*); its counterpart, the written vocal fugue, left the composer time for reflection, but had to be written with the only aid of a sketch of the exposition, given by the master. The first could bestow to its practitioners an unparalleled fluency in improvisation, but perhaps led to a certain neglect of the strict voice leading. The practice of the second awarded the student with a flawless command of a full-voiced texture, but charged the beginners with the responsibility of planning all compositional choices (tonal plan, form, motivic play, and so on).

The growing interest in the *partimento* tradition has recently resulted in an increasing number of publications dealing, more or less directly, with *partimento*-fugues. All these works, however, focus on the German *partimento*-fugues, with only fleeting (and generic) mentions of the existence of another, earlier tradition rooted in Naples. Table 1 is a first attempt to counterbalance the German-oriented emphasis of the current literature on *partimento*-fugue. It is a partial list of some of the surviving sources of Neapolitan *partimento*-fugues (a complete list is at the moment not realistic since many libraries are still to be searched).[5] The sheer size of the Neapolitan legacy clearly surpasses the hitherto known sources in all other traditions. More impressive is its continuity: beginning with Rocco Greco (born about 1650), and finishing with Pietro Platania, who died in 1907, the Neapolitans had been using *partimento*-fugues for over two centuries without interruption.

---

4. Leonardo Leo, *Istituzioni o regole del contrappunto del Sig.re Leonardo Leo. 1792.* Naples: Biblioteca del Conservatorio S. Pietro a Majella, MS 22.2.6-3. This work, of which several copies exist, is discussed in Alessandro Abbate, "Due autori per un testo di contrappunto di scuola napoletana: Leonardo Leo e Michele Gabellone", in: *Studi Musicali 36* (2007), pp. 123-159.
5. In Table 1 the libraries are designates according to the standard RISM sigla.

Table 1. *The Neapolitan partimento-fugue: a partial list in chronological order.*

Early XVIII century

Rocco Greco (ca.1650–before 1718) — **Gaetano Greco** (1657–1728)
About 60 fugues, fughette and versetti in the following sources: I-Mc
Z 16-13; I-Mc N 49-1; I-Nc Ms 45.1.65 (olim 33.2.9); I-Nc 33.2.3
(olim Musica Strumentale 2850); I-Nc. Rari 1.9.15(2) I-Rsc A.400.

[Nicola] Fago (1677–1745)
7 *partimento*-fugues in I-Nc MS 2066 (olim 24.1.2).

Mid XVIII century

Francesco Durante (1684-1755)
About 25 *partimento*-fugues in different sources, such as I-Nc Roche
A. 5. 6; I-Nc MS 1908; I-Nc 22.1.14; I-PESc Rari ms. II 8; I-PESc
Rari ms. c. 13; I-Mc Noseda Th. C. 107; I-Mc Noseda Th.C.133;
I-Mc Noseda Th.C.134; I-Bc EE. 171.

Leonardo Leo (1694–1744)
10 *partimento*-fugues in various sources, such as I-Nc 22.2.6-5; I-Nc
22.1.26; I-PESc Rari c 12.
19 fugues in I-Mc Noseda Th.c.113.
21 fugues in I-MC 3-D-18/5 (in part they coincide with the other
sources).

Andrea Basili (1705–1777)
Musica universale armonico-pratica, Venezia 1776, A collection of 24
preludes and fugues in all keys: 10 fugues are written as *partimento*.

Late XVIII century

Carlo Cotumacci (1709–1785)
18 *partimento*-fugues in various sources, such as I-Nc S.7.12;
I-Nc.O(C).3.40; I-Nc 34.2.1; I-BGi.X 8590; I-Mc Noseda Th.c.106.

Nicola Sala (1713-1801)
Circa one hundred *partimento*-fugues in various sources, such as I-Mc
Noseda Th.116 b; I-Nc 46.1.34; I-PESc Rari Ms.II.20.
(also in Alexandre-Étienne Choron, *Principes de composition des écoles
d'Italie*, Paris 1808.)

Giacomo Insanguine, alias Monopoli (1728-1795)
13 *partimento*-fugues in I-Mc Noseda Th-c 116/a.

Saverio Valente (1767?-1811?)
7 *partimento*-fugues in I-Mc Noseda Q. 13.17.

Fedele Fenaroli (1730-1818)
60 *partimento*-fugues in books V and VI of *Partimenti o sia basso
numerato* (various editions).

Early XIX century

Giacomo Tritto (1733-1824)
9 *partimento*-fugues in *Scuola di contrappunto o sia Teorica musicale*,
Milano, Artaria 1819.
12 fughe-*partimento* in *Partimenti e regole generali*, Milano, Artaria
1821.

Niccolò Zingarelli (1752-1837)
Partimenti del signor maestro don Nicolò Zingarelli, Milano, Ricordi,
n.ed. 6823-6824 [ca. 1830].
49 *partimento*-fugues: 27 in Book I, 22 in Book II.

Mid — to late XIX century

Pietro Raimondi (1786-1853)
Bassi imitati e fugati divisi in tre libri, Milano, Ricordi [1876].

Pietro Platania (1828-1907)
Corso completo di fughe e canoni, Milano, Ricordi 1871.
*Trattato d'armonia seguito da un corso completo di contrappunto dal
corale al fugato e partimenti analoghi*, Milano, Ricordi 1872.

The purpose of the present article is to offer a survey of this genre in Naples, from the beginning in the early eighteenth century to the early nineteenth century; and, at the same time, to discuss some aspects of the *partimento*-fugue realization with specific reference to the Neapolitan tradition.[6] As representative of the transformations of this genre, I have chosen two authors from the early eighteenth century, Gaetano Greco and Nicola Fago; two from the mid-eighteenth century, Leonardo Leo and Francesco Durante; and Fedele Fenaroli as the most important master in the period between the two centuries. It goes without saying that this is only an introductory essay; it does not claim to summarize in few pages a bicentennial tradition. I hope, though, to give an idea of the fundamental principles of this practice.

1.

EARLY EIGHTEENTH CENTURY: THE GRECO BROTHERS AND NICOLA FAGO

GAETANO & ROCCO GRECO

The Greco brothers were major figures in the Neapolitan musical life between the end of the seventeenth and the beginning of the eighteenth century. Rocco Greco (ca. 1650–before 1718) studied at the Poveri di Gesù Cristo, and taught the violin at the same conservatory from 1677 to 1695, when he became first violin at the royal chapel of Naples. His younger brother Gaetano (1627–1728) studied at the Poveri di Gesù Cristo conservatory with Gennaro Ursino and, possibly, with Alessandro Scarlatti. In 1677 he began his teaching career in the same conservatory as secondo maestro, and from 1696 as maestro di cappella. Among his students were Giuseppe Porsile, Nicola Porpora, Leonardo Vinci and Domenico Scarlatti (the presence of Pergolesi is uncertain). His successor was Francesco Durante. Both brothers wrote *partimenti*: those by Rocco

---

6. For a general introduction to *partimento* realization see Giorgio Sanguinetti, "The Realization of *Partimenti*: An Introduction," in: *Journal of Music Theory* 51/1 (2007), pp. 51–83.

survive in only one source, while there are at least five manuscripts of Gaetano's *partimenti*.

The *partimento*-fugues of Rocco and Gaetano Greco are short (twenty or thirty bars) and derive from the Organ versetto. Their standard format usually includes a complete exposition, followed by two or three middle entries separated by episodes, and concluding with a cadential section. Example 1 shows three short, imitative *partimenti* from the manuscript Noseda Z16-13 in the library of the conservatory of Milan, a codex that includes 73 *partimenti*. They exhibit a remarkable variety in the treatment of imitation: respectively, at the fifth (no. 27), fourth (no. 29) and octave (no. 33).[7]

Example 1. Gaetano Greco, three versetti (from the MS Noseda Z16-13):
a) no. 27 in C minor

7. The source is: Partimenti per cembalo. N. 4 – Del Sig.r Gaetano Greco. Milan: Biblioteca del Conservatorio G. Verdi, Noseda Z 16-13. In my transcription of numbers 27, 29 and 33 I have normalized the barring, which in the manuscript is inconsistent and, in no. 29, almost non-existent.

Example 1. Gaetano Greco, three versetti (from the MS Noseda Z16-13): b) no. 29 in G major; c) no. 33 in B flat major.

In addition to the interval of the imitation, these three short compositions differ in many other ways. The entries of no. 27 are arranged in couples, with reversed order (soprano-alto, m. 1; bass-tenor, mm. 4–5). After the first episode (mm. 7–9) the mid entries are arranged sequentially (mm. 9–15). A second episode (mm. 15–19) leads to the last appearance of the main thematic idea in the cadential section (mm. 19-22).

Example 2: Gaetano Greco, versetto no. 33 (from the MS Noseda Z16-13) realized.

The exposition of no. 29 exhibits what will become the favorite solution of late eighteenth century *partimento*-fugue. The entries are arranged in descending order, SATB, and every new voice is announced by its own clef. When the exposition ends (m. 8), a two-bars connection brings to a stretto-like entry (mm. 10-11) leading to the cadence. The main difficulty in playing this *partimento* is to find an appropriate upper counterpoint to the entries. However, since the *partimento* itself carries out the rhythmic and thematic activity, the accompaniment may also be in a simple continuo style.[8]

---

8. The performer may complete the stretto adding a third entry in the accompaniment in m. 12, following the ascending order C–D (in the bass)–E.

In realizing no. 33 the performer meets a different situation. Here the second entry, in the alto voice, abruptly breaks the continuity of the melodic line of the first entry, which calls for its completion: a chordal accompaniment is clearly unsuitable here. In addition, the continuo-like figures in m. 2 do not indicate chords, but a melodic line in the soprano moving in parallel thirds with the notated part. This *partimento* therefore requires a contrapuntal realization, like the one suggested in Example 2.

This example points to a first major difference between the Neapolitan and the German tradition, namely the importance of melodic continuity. Whereas German *partimento*-fugues allow melodically discontinuous realizations, often in form of block chords textures, the Neapolitan generally required a melodically flu-ent realization. Interestingly, the melodic connections are implied in the *partimenti* themselves (as Example 3 makes clear), and are obvious even in absence of a written realization.[9]

NICOLA FAGO

The seven surviving fugues by Nicola Fago (also known as "the Tarantino" after his birthplace) are large works in vocal style alter-nating tutti and soli. They appear in one of the only two known *par-timento* manuscipts attributed to Fago, a short codex of 15 pages.[10] Although few in number, Fago's fugues exhibit unique features, which may shed light on the late seventeenth or early eighteenth century *partimento* practice. Some fugues make explicit reference to liturgical texts: *Kyrie* (no. 2) and *Cum sanctu spiritu* (no. 5). All seven fugues have added performance instructions (Tutti; Solo; Basso; Sanza Organo; Serrato; For.[te]) suggesting that these fugues may be either the *basso seguente* part for a piece of vocal music, or

---

9. The German tradition of partimento-fugue is discussed in William Renwick, *The Langloz Manuscript. Fugal Improvisation Through Figured Bass*, New York 2001; and, more recently, in Bruno Gingras, "Partimento-fugue in Eighteenth-Century Germany: A Bridge Between Thoroughbass Lessons and Fugal Composition," in: *Eighteenth-Century Music* 5/1 (2008), pp. 51-74.
10. *Fughe del Sig. Fago per uso di me Giuseppe Mirone. Nell'anno 1813*. Naples: Biblioteca del Conservatorio S. Pietro a Majella, MS 2066.

that they are *partimenti* drawn from pre-existant vocal scores. In all cases, there is little doubt that these fugues have a practical, rather than pedagogical, function. Besides, like the Greco *versetti*, they have clearly been written for an organist, who must have used them during his service in the church. All these circumstances point to the conclusion that, in the early years of the eighteenth century (and perhaps even before), the *partimento* was used as notational shorthand with the purpose to support organists in their improvisations.

Example 3. Nicola Fago, Fuga no. 2 (Kyrie) from I-Nc MS. 2066 (reproduction of pp. 3-4 of the manuscript).

2.

MID-EIGHTEENTH CENTURY:
LEONARDO LEO & FRANCESCO DURANTE

Despite the number and the sophisticated musical quality of the *partimenti* written in the early eighteenth century by composers like Pasquini, Scarlatti, Fago and the Grecos, the standard model of the Neapolitan *partimento* was established by the two great masters born around the end of the seventeenth century: Francesco Durante (1684–1755) and Leonardo Leo (1694–1744). The *partimenti* of Leo and Durante definitively abandon the format of the organ *versetto* and adopt a moderate length comparable to that of a movement of a sonata or a concerto. They also exhibit an impressive variety in form and texture, and cover most, if not all, of the keyboard styles and genres in use during the first half of the eighteenth century. There are no significant differences between the style of the *partimenti* of Leo and Durante. Leo perhaps showed more inclination towards concertante texture, and Durante towards galante style; for what counterpoint is concerned, both authors wrote equally masterful *partimento*-fugues. Any discussion about stylistic differences in Leo's and Durante's *partimenti*, however, is doomed to uncertainty because of the frequent double attributions. Often the same *partimento* appears in collections ascribed to Leo as well as in others ascribed to Durante. Since the autographs are lost, there is no way to determine the authorship with certainty. Perhaps one could say that the fugues whose attribution to Durante is prevalent are closer to the *sonata da chiesa* style, while those bearing more consistently the attribution to Leo often exhibit elements of ritornello form. However, a manuscript in the Milan conservatory library attributed to Leo contains several *partimento*-fugues in strict vocal style.[11]

LEONARDO LEO

A fine example of *partimento*-fugue mingled with concerto form is no. 40 from a manuscript kept in the library of conservatory of

---

11. *Partimenti numerati del Sig.r Maestro Leonardo Leo.* Milan: Biblioteca del Conservatorio G. Verdi, Noseda Th.c.113.

Pesaro: its attribution to Leo is confirmed by other manuscripts.[12] Example 4 gives a complete transcription of the *partimento*, with formal labels added. The piece is a large concertante fugue spanning more than one hundred fifty bars (almost three times the longest fugue in the Langloz manuscript) based on a steady pace in quarter notes, except for the the last bars of those sections ending with a cadence: in those places the performer should provide the missing quarters in order to restore the rhythmic continuity.

	Sections of the fugue	Measures	Begins	Ends	T/S	Sections of the Concerto
block 1	Exposition	1-11	I	V/I	s/t	Ritornello 1 (opening)
	Episode 1	11-22	V/I	V/III	soli	Soli 1
	Episode 1a	22-33	III	III	tutti	Cadential
block 2	Entry 1	33-43	III	V/III	s/t	Ritornello 2
	Episode 2	43-56	V/III	V/IV	soli	Soli 2
	Episode 2a	56-63	IV	IV	tutti	Cadential
block 3	Entry 2	63-67	IV	IV	soli	Ritornello 3 (abridged)
	Episode 3	67-77	IV	V/vii	soli	Soli 3
	Episode 3a	78-84	vii	vii	tutti	Cadential
block 4	Entry 3	84-94	vii	v/vii	s/t	Ritornello 4
	Episode 4	94-107	v/vii	V/VI	soli	Soli 4
	Episode 4a	108-117	VI	VI	tutti	Cadential
block 5	Entry 4 (stretto)	117-127	VI	V/VI	s/t	Ritornello 5 (abridged)
	Episode 5 (stretto)	127-136	V/VI	IV	soli	Soli 5
	Episode 5a	136-142	IV	I	tutti	Cadential
block 6	Entry 5 (complete exposition)	142-159	I	I	tutti	Ritornello 6 (closing)

Table 2. Form chart of Leo's partimento *no. 40 (from I-PESc Rari Ms.c.12).*

Table 2 gives a chart of the form of this piece: in this table the outermost columns indicate, at the left, the sections of the fugue and, at the right, the corresponding sections of the concerto form. The other columns indicate the bars, the harmonic degree on which the sections

---

12. *Partimenti del Mº Leonardo Leo.* Pesaro, Biblioteca del Conservatorio G. Rossini, Rari MS.c.12.

begin and end, and the alternation of tutti/soli. The tutti/soli quality is determined by the clefs: a high clef (C or G) corresponds to the soli, the basso clef with continuo figures corresponds to the tutti.

Example 4: Leonardo Leo, partimento *no. 40 from manuscript I-PESc Rari Ms.c.12.*

(*example 4: continuation*)

As it is customary for *partimento*-fugues, Leo's fugues in concerto form always begin with the subject in the high register, in soprano clef or in G clef. After the entrance of the subject, the other voices usually enter in the descending order SATB.[13] In this case, however, the answer is not in the alto voice, as usual, but — rather surprisingly — in the bass: the continuo figures indicate that it must be played with a full texture. This uncommon procedure is clearly intended as mimicking the beginning of an opening tutti in a concerto, with the violins answered by the tutti; as a result, the exposition consist only of two entries, for a fugue that obviously has more than two voices.[14]

After that, the exposition episodes and middle entries alternate regularly, like soli and tutti in a concerto: subject/answer entries take the place of the ritornello, and episodes alternate tutti and soli, connecting the different transpositions of the ritornelli/entries. More specifically, the form of this piece is based on five varied and transposed repetitions (the last one is modified) of the initial block consisting in three modules: a subject/answer thematic entry, a soli episode and a cadential tutti. The thematic content of the modules remains the same in each repetition, but with significant modifications. For example, in the second repetition of the block (mm. 63-84) the entry module has no tutti, but two soli with subject/answer in stretto (mm. 63-67, with alto clef). The fourth block (mm. 117-143) similarly opens with a stretto entry (mm. 117-121) this time followed by the tutti; the stretto idea infiltrates also the following soli episode (mm. 127-136) and the last module (tutti, mm. 136-143), for the first time, is based on the subject. Finally, the closing block (mm. 143-158) consists of a final statement of subject/answer in descending order in all voices, and replaces (in a very unorthodox way) the missing complete exposition in the beginning of the fugue. Concerning the tonal aspects, in each block the first module is relatively stable, the central one is unstable (modulating), and

---

13. Other examples of this kind are are nos. 11 and 19 in the Pesaro manuscript. The descending order of the entries is typical of *partimento* fugue, because it allows the performer to improvise the counterpoint above a lower part, which is easier than improvising a bass below a given part. See also William Renwick, *The Langloz Manuscript — Fugal Improvisation through Figured Bass*, Oxford 2001, p. 15.

14. Other instances of this kind in the Pesaro manuscript: nos. 28, 30 & 41.

the third is stable, with the only exception of block 5. All diatonic degrees are explored, except the second and fifth. While the second is clearly avoided because of its diminished triad, the avoidance of a transposition on the dominant seems to be a characteristic feature of the Neapolitan fugues, also of the vocal type.[15]

In Neapolitan *partimento*-fugues there are often extended passages with a two-voice texture in a rather high register, as happens in mm. 11-22 (and parallel passages) of Example 4. In such cases a question might arise: should one play these passages as written, or complete them by adding a bass below the *partimento*. The first option would result in a thin, sometimes awkward sonority, the second seems to be contrary to the generally accepted identification of the *partimento* with a bass. As a matter of fact, the few definitions of *partimento* found in Neapolitan sources from the seventeenth to the nineteenth century, always take the term *partimento* as a synonym for bass. Coherently with this definition, the addition of a new voice below the *partimento* is impossible; an idea that Heinichen seems to agree with in the chapter on Bassetti in *Der Generalbass in der Composition*.[16] A totally different opinion was expressed by Karl Gustav Fellerer in *Der Partimento-Spieler*,[17] the only book on this topic published during the twentieth century. Fellerer explicitly allows this possibility when the bass is omitted in favor of a thematically relevant statement:

> In such cases the bass voice may be added, exactly as with any other voice. In a *partimento*, as opposed to the usual thoroughbass, the written voice is not always also the lowest voice.[18]

More recently, William Renwick and Bruno Gingras mention the possibility of adding a bass below to the *partimento* voice during sequential passages. The additions, however, never involves thematic

---

15. See Gaetano Stella, "Partimenti in the Age of Romanticism: Raimondi, Platania, and Boucheron," in: *Journal of Music Theory* 51/1 (2007), pp. 161–186.

16. Johann David Heinichen, *Der Generalbass in der Komposition*, Dresden 1728.

17. Karl Gustav Fellerer, *Der Partimento-Spieler*, Leipzig 1940.

18. Die Baßstimme wird in solchen Fällen wie die übrigen ergänzt. Die im Partimento ausgeschriebene Stimme ist im Gegensatz zum gewöhnlichen Generalbaß also nicht immer Grundstimme. ibid, p. 8.

statements, but only accompaniments, and are to be intended as "the exception rather than the norm."[19] Until now, I have never found a *partimento*-fugue that invites the performer to play a thematic statement *below* the notated line (the addition of a thematic statement *above* the *partimento* is rather common) and I doubt that this could ever have been a possibility in this tradition. In general, with regard to the addition of a part below the *partimento*, one encounters the following two cases: the first is relatively common, the second quite rare.

- Case A. A bass may be added below a free passage (usually, a sequential episode, or a cadential passage);
- Case B. A bass might be added below a thematic statement.

Example 5. mm. 11-22 of Leo no. 49 with bass added.

Concerning Case A, I invite the reader to consider Example 4 again. Episode 1 (mm. 11 to 22) begins with a free imitation on the rhythm of the subject, but in m. 19 the rhythmic pace suddenly comes to a halt, followed by four bars of two-voice counterpoint in half-notes. If we play this passage the way it is written, the result is rather poor. First of all, there is no reason to interrupt the rhythmic continuity of

---

19. Bruno Gingras, "Partimento-fugue in Eighteenth-Century Germany: A Bridge Between Thoroughbass Lessons and Fugal Composition", in: *Eighteenth-Century Music* 5/1 (2008), p. 64. Similar cases are discussed in William Renwick, *The Langloz Manuscript — Fugal Improvisation through Figured Bass*, Oxford 2001, pp. 17, 59, 65.

the piece at this point; secondly, the section would end with a weak contrapuntal cadence. These problems are instantly solved with the addition of a bass line moving in quarter-notes below the notated *partimento*: the rhythmic continuity is restored, and the solo section ends with a strong, authentic cadence.

FRANCESCO DURANTE

In the example just discussed, a general principle of *partimento* realization is at work, I will call it the "principle of complementarity." The idea behind this principle is that a *partimento* is the notated part of a musical whole. In order to get the whole we must reconstruct the missing part in such a way that it will complement the partimento. In Example 5 the principle of complementarity applies to the rhythmic continuity. Most *partimenti* follow a steady, uniform rhythmic pace. When the regularity of the pace is interrupted, the performer must restore it with the addition of a rhythmically complementary voice. As we will see later, the principle of complementarity applies not only to rhythm, but also to other aspects of the realization, particularly to the identification of "hidden" entries in a *partimento*-fugue.

The second case is more difficult. In comparison to the relatively easy task of adding a bass to some standardized cadential point, adding a bass under a thematic statement involves a greater contrapuntal skill. Still, there are *partimenti* where this technique is very appropriate. A rather extreme case is a *partimento* generally ascribed to Durante, and titled in several manuscripts Fuga no. 2 (but there is also an attribution to Nicola Sala). This *partimento* is shown in Example 6.[20]

---

20. As principal source I have consulted I-PESc Rari Ms.C.13 pp. 256–7. Other sources are: I-Mc Noseda Th.c.123 pp. 207–8; I-Nc 34-2-3 cc. 117v-118; I-Bc E.E. 171, p. 122). This partimento appears also in a collection ascribed to Nicola Sala (*Fughe del M.tro Nicola Sala*, I-Mc Th.c.116b, no. 17). It is included as no. 97 in the only currently available paper edition: Giuseppe A. Pastore (ed.), *Francesco Durante, Bassi e Fughe. Un manuale inedito per riscoprire la vera prassi esecutiva della Scuola Napoletana del Settecento*, Padova 2003. Unfortunately, the text of this edition is not entirely correct. This *partimento* is not yet included in the *Monuments of Partimenti* online edition.

Fugue no. 2 is a rare instance of a *partimento*-fugue in organ style with an ascending exposition, in which the *partimento* line moves from one voice to another following the order BTAS.[21] Another, more common possibility for a *partimento*-fugue with ascending exposition is that the *partimento* always follows the bass part, and the position of the entries are either left unmarked or are signaled in some ways. For example, in a fugue ascribed to Durante in the manuscript I-GR It.125 (c. 33v), the entries are indicated with the names of the voices (*Solo; Tenore; Alto; Canto*). Another usage is in a manuscript in the Montecassino Library, where fugue no. 2 bears the caption "enter the voices from the bass to the treble, and upper treble" (*Entrare con le parti dal grave all'acuto, e sopra acuto*).[22]

Turning back to Example 6, the subject itself is quite unusual: its first half consists of a chromatic ascent from $\hat{5}$ to $\hat{8}$, followed by a diatonic cadential motion. In the next-to-last measure a second voice enters, whose only purpose is to create a $\hat{8}-\hat{7}$-$\hat{8}$ suspension as an accompaniment to the cadence. Accompanied subjects are not rare in late baroque fugues. As a rule, Neapolitan *partimento*-fugues don't have a real countersubject: the accompaniment to the subject is open to modifications, and usually is not in double counterpoint (as far as the voices enter in descending order, this is not a necessity). When a fugue has a real countersubject, it appears together with the first entry of the subject, not with the answer (as in the standard Bach procedure). This kind of fugue is called double fugue, or *fuga col contra soggetto*.[23] However, this added voice has no thematic relevance, so it is obviously not a countersubject. Its only purpose is to make explicit the voice-leading and harmonic implications of the cadential motion.

---

21. This *partimento* appears also in some collections of partimenti ascribed to Leo, such as manuscript 3-D-18/5, in Montecassino, Biblioteca del Monumento Nazionale.
22. *Fughe n. 21 del Sig. Leonardo Leo*, I-MC 3-D-18/3 c. 2r.
23. In his treatise on counterpoint, Giacomo Tritto stipulates that in this kind of fugues the exposition has no more than two entries. Giacomo Tritto, *Scuola di contrappunto ossia teorica musicale*, Milan 1816, p. 31.

Example 6. Durante [?] Fugue no. 2.

Example 7. Durante, Fuga no. 2, realized.

(example 7: continuation)

As it happens, the exposition as a whole is quite a paradox. Whereas the first entry of the subject is marked solo, the first answer bears figures, at least in many sources. This leads to the curious circumstance that the tenor entry is accompanied by other voices (two, according to the figures) *above* it, while the bass remains silent. I don't really think that these figures are to be taken literally. Quite possibly, the copyists have mechanically reproduced the figures on every occurrence of the answer. But, even if we take the figures as authentic, a two voice realization is also possible, and the result is very close to a *fuga con il contra soggetto*.

After the second entry, however, the exposition continues to soar, until the fifth entry (mm. 21-24) reaches the extreme high register (c³). If one plays this exposition the way it is written, the effect is nonsensical: the voices drop out as soon as a new one enters, leaving every new entry bare and unaccompanied. One might speculate that the accompaniment is intended to be played above the entries, as in mm. 6-11, but I doubt it. The continuous ascent through the registers makes it illogical to play anything above the written notes. In addition, the general effect of such an exposition would sound empty and unsatisfying. Therefore, in my opinion, one or more lower voices must be added below the *partimento* through the exposition from bar 12 to 24, and in all other places of this fugue where a bass is appropriate.

Example 7 shows my interpretation of this fugue. In order to help the reader, the realization is written with smaller noteheads. After the exposition, I have added a new bass only in the second episode (the cadences in mm. 42 and 46), and completed the alto line in mm. 49-50. The entries in mm. 56-64 give the opportunity for a stretto, and for an optional extra voice in the bass in mm. 59-64 (this new bass is not necessary for an harpsichord or piano performance, but very appropriate on the organ). As always, it should be kept in mind that this is not "the" solution, but just one (not necessarily the best) of a potentially unlimited number of possible realizations.

3.

LATE EIGHTEENTH – EARLY NINETEENTH CENTURY: FEDELE FENAROLI

Fedele Fenaroli was undoubtably the most influential Neapolitan teacher in the period from the end of the eighteenth to the beginning of the nineteenth century. Born in Lanciano (Abruzzi) in 1730, he studied with Durante at the S. Maria di Loreto conservatory where he started his teaching career in 1762 as *secondo maestro*. In more than half a century (he virtually taught until his death in 1818) Fenaroli had a huge number of students (legend has it that they reached the astounding number of nine thousand!), among them Domenico Cimarosa, Nicolò Zingarelli, Nicola Manfroce, Saverio Mercadante, and Vincenzo Lavigna, the future teacher of Giuseppe Verdi.[24]

Fugue	Entries	Measures	Begins	Ends	Sonata	
Exposition	SRSR	1 - 15	i	v	Exposition	Main theme
First episode		15 – 23	v	V/v		Transition
Counterexposition	RSRS	23 – 36	v	i		Subordinate theme
Second episode		36 – 61	i	V	Development	
Middle entries	SRSR	61 – 72	i	v	Recapitulation	Main theme
Third episode		72 – 80	v	V/v		Transition
Stretti	RS	80 – 84	v	i		Subordinate theme
Fourth episode		84 – 90	i	V	Coda	
Pedal point & cadence		90 – 98	V	i		Closing cadence

Table 3. Formal outline of fugue no. 1 from Fenaroli's fifth book of partimenti.

Fenaroli's *partimento*-related output consists of a short treatise, the *Regole musicali per i principianti di cembalo*, first published in 1775, and a collection of *partimenti* arranged in six books. They circulated in manuscript for several decades before being published

---

24. See Rosa Cafiero, *"La musica è di nuova specie, si compone senza regole": Fenaroli e la tradizione didattica napoletana tra Sette e Ottocento*. Paper read at the conference *Fedele Fenaroli. Il didatta e il compositore* (Lanciano, 15–16 November 2008).

for the first time in 1814 in Paris in an expensive two-language edition. Both *Regole* and *partimenti* have been continuously reissued under different names by many publishers until the beginning of the twentieth century. Books four and five of Fenaroli include 60 *partimento*-fugues. Table 3 gives a chart of the form of the first fugue from Fenaroli's Book V, the fugue is shown in Example 8. The formal outline of this fugue is by and large valid for all Fenaroli fugues, except for those *col contra soggetto*.

The formal plan of this fugue bears clear affinities with the sonata form. The first episode shares some elements with the transition, like the $\hat{4}$–$\#\hat{4}$ motion in the bass and the close on the dominant of V; the counterexposition with reversed order of entries (ASAS) takes the place of the subordinate theme. As a rule, the first two entries of the counterexposition are "hidden", that is, they are not indicated on the *partimento*, and the performer must find the right spot to have them enter. The second episode is much larger than the first, and shows some characteristics of the development: it ends usually with a half-cadence on V or III, followed with a caesura. The next series of entries is usually abbreviated, but the order of the entries is the same as in the exposition (SASA). It takes the place of the recapitulation, and is followed by the repetition of the first episode, which leads to the stretti and is followed by the final cadential close.

Example 8. Fugue no. 1 from Fenaroli's fifth book of partimenti.

(example 8: continuation)

Example 9. Fenaroli, Fugue no. 1 realized for keyboard by Angelo Catelani.

4.

A NINETEENTH CENTURY KEYBOARD
REALIZATION

Fenaroli's fugue offers an excellent occasion for dealing with another relevant problem concerning the realization of *partimento*-fugues, namely the number of voices and their arrangement. Should the texture be free or strict? Is the performer supposed to play the bass with the left hand and the chords with the right, or should he/she adopt an "open" texture, with two voices in each hand? Should the performer merely "fill in" the harmony, or should he/she aim to a contrapuntal fabric? [25]

One might expect to find an answer to this problem (as well as to others) in early realizations of *partimenti*, or in treatises; perhaps in those manuscripts bearing titles such as *Regole di partimenti* or *Maniera di ben suonare il cembalo* that survive in large numbers in Italian libraries. As a matter of fact, there is no treatise explaining how to realize a *partimento*-fugue; and the *Regole* manuscript only deals with the elementary realization of unfigured basses. Luckily, some examples of eighteenth century realizations of *partimenti* (but not yet of *partimento*-fugues) have recently began to surface, and their number will probably increase in the future. At present, the earliest known realizations of *partimento*-fugues (by Angelo Catelani, Emanuele Guarnaccia, Gennaro Bonamici, Placido Mandanici, Vincenzo Fiocchi and Vincenzo Lavigna) belong to the first half of nineteenth century, and deal exclusively with fugues by Fenaroli. Judging from these sources, one might infer that the style of the keyboard realizations was supposed to be rather free. An authoritative source is manuscript F. 370 in the Estense library in Modena.[26] The

---

25. According to the extant sources, in the German tradition the realization of partimento-fugues often followed the free texture typical of the accompaniment of a figured bass. A well-known example is Heinichen's realization of a *partimento*-fugue in Johann David Heinichen, *Der General-Bass in der Composition*, Dresden 1728. See George J. Buelow, *Thoroughbass Accompaniment according to Johann David Heinichen*, Lincoln and London 1986, pp. 208-11.

26. [Angelo Catelani] *Fenaroli, Partimenti disposti secondo i principii della Scuola di Napoli, con Appendice del M° Durante*, Modena: Biblioteca Estense, Mus. F. 370.

manuscript was compiled by Angelo Catelani, an influential musician and teacher who studied with Niccolò Zingarelli around 1830. His realization of the beginning of Fenaroli's fugue no. 1 is shown in Example 9.

Catelani realizes the entire exposition (with four entries) with three voices only. He also adds a third voice (an upper pedal point) above the answer, where Fenaroli had written a single voice counterpoint. All successive entries are transpositions of the second, always with the same three-voice texture; a fourth voice is added at the beginning of the episode, but only to complete the harmony. This manner of writing seems to contradict the very nature of fugue, whereas the growing weight of the texture during the exposition, and its sudden relief in the episodes, are part of the aesthetic of the genre. This contradiction, however, is partly counterbalanced by the growing intensification of sonority produced through the alternation of subject and answers in downward direction.

5.

A DIFFERENT STYLE OF REALIZATION:
THE *DISPOSIZIONE*

Around 1825 Ricordi published an annotated edition of Fenaroli's *partimenti* edited by Emanuele Guarnaccia, a virtually unknown musician who seems to have been active in Venice in the first decade of the nineteenth century. Guarnaccia's edition is unique in that it offers a page-to-page realization of books 4, 5 and 6, together with a text that differs completely from the original *Regole*. In doing so, Guarnaccia patently plagiarized Catelani for the realizations, and Imbimbo for the more theoretical side of his text. However, the original parts offer interesting insight into the *partimento* practice: one is an example of Fenaroli's first fugue with a realization written in open score on four staves (the first 23 measures are shown in Example 10). The Neapolitan called this kind of realization a *disposizione* (this term could be translated as "setting").[27]

In the *disposizione* the exposition proceeds with a regular increase of the number of voices. Between the staves Guarnaccia has also added some labels reflecting the Neapolitan terminology. The term *attacco* indicates the short appendix added to the subject whose purpose is to lead to (*attaccare*) the answer. Notice also the use of the term *contrasoggetto*; in this *disposizione* Guarnaccia treats Fenaroli's counterpoint as a real countersubject. Later he will introduce a new countersubject (*nuovo controsoggetto*), and towards the end of the fugue the first will be brought in again. These *disposizioni* witness an alternative use of the *partimenti*: in addition to be a guide for a more or less improvised performance, they also were used as compositional matrices for written polyphonic pieces.

---

27. The term *disposizione* actually covers a larger spectrum of meanings. A *disposizione* can be based on *partimento*, or be a free composition. Differently from a *partimento* realization, in a *disposizione* the number of voices (usually from two to four) is obligate, as in a strict counterpoint exercise. Interesting sources are the *disposizioni* written by Vincenzo Lavigna (Verdi's composition teacher) under the supervision of Fenaroli, see Giorgio Sanguinetti, "Diminution and Harmony-oriented Counterpoint in Late Eighteenth Century Naples: Vincenzo Lavigna's Studies with Fedele Fenaroli," in Oliver Schwab-Felisch, Michael Polth & Hartmut Fladt (eds.), *Schenkerian Analysis—Analyse nach Heinrich Schenker. Bericht über den internationalen Schenker-Kongreß in Berlin, Sauen und Mannheim, 4.-12. Juni 2004*, Hildesheim (forthcoming). Also some collections of partimenti are titled disposizioni, perhaps they were primarily intended as bases for this kind of written realizations, see, for example, Carlo Cotumacci, *Disposizioni a tre, e quattro parti, ossiano Partimenti*, Milan: Biblioteca del Conservatorio G. Verdi, Noseda E.66.16.

Example 10. Fenaroli, Fugue no. 1 realized as disposizione *by Emanuele Guarnaccia.*

(example 10: continuation)

6.

THE "HIDDEN ENTRIES"

The final aspect of *partimento*-fugue performance I will deal with, concerns what I call the "hidden entries". The performer of a *partimento*-fugue may face two different situations concerning the entries of subject and/or answer. They can be stated in the *partimento*, in which case the task of the performer consists in adding the accompaniment. In other cases, the *partimento* gives the accompaniment, and the performer must enter the subject (or the answer) in the appropriate spots. In this latter case, there are still two possibilities: either the *partimento* makes clear the position of the entries, or they are entirely left to the performer's perspicacity. Concerning the first possibility, the *maestri* have found several systems to help the performer: clefs changings, pitch names added above the score (among other, Händel used this system), the names of the voices in which the entries are expected to appear, fully written notations such as *entra la fuga* (used by Pasquini) or imitazione and abbreviations (the most widely used is "imit"). Often there are no indications, the performer must find the correct position without any help, just scanning the contrapuntal possibilities of the *partimento*. This task is obviously facilitated by the presence of a fixed countersubject, as in many German *partimento*-fugues, or in the Neapolitan *fughe col contra soggetto*. In those cases, the performer has to memorize the countersubject and place the entries accordingly. More frequently, however, Neapolitan *partimento*-fugues have no obligate countersubject, and bear no shorthand of the entries, I call these entries "hidden". In general, the Neapolitan masters were favorably disposed towards "hidden" thematic entries, for example, Leo, Durante and Fenaroli used them regularly. Some other authors, like Paisiello, Sala and Zingarelli, used to show the places where the imitation should occur. For example, in his *Regole per bene accompagnare il partimento*, Paisiello took great care to make all imitations explicit in the partimenti written for the Grand Duchess Maria Feodorovna of Russia — but, after all, the dedicatee was not a professional.[28]

---

28. Giovanni Paisiello, *Regole per bene accompagnare il Partimento, o sia il Basso Fondamentale* [...], St. Petersburg, 1782.

How precisely the correct placement of a hidden entry can be found in a *partimento*? As I have already observed in my comment to table 3, Fenaroli generally places two "hidden" entries at the beginning of the counterexposition, ordered as ASAS. In the exposition, Fenaroli usually composes a "neutral" (i.e. not thematically pregnant) counterpoint as accompaniment for the thematic entries, and places it above the *partimento*. Since this accompaniment is typically not in double counterpoint, scanning the *partimento* for its occurrences would bring no results. The only possibility consists in what I have already called the "principle of complementarity". Before explaining the application of this principle to the "hidden" entries, I will offer other two examples, again from the first fugue of book V. Example 11 shows the counterexposition of the fugue, where two hidden entries in succession occur.

Example 11. Fenaroli, Fugue no. 1 partimento only: hidden entries (mm. 23-30).

In absence of a countersubject, no thematic or motivic hint can help the search for the "hidden entries", so at this point, the *partimento* is totally different from the *fauxbourdon* used in the exposition. However, any student trained according to the principles of the Neapolitan school would immediately recognize in the bass line in mm. 23-30 a slightly embellished version of the descending minor scale according to the "Rule of the Octave" — a rule that was inculcated in the minds (and hands) of the students from the onset of their studies. Example 12 shows the relation between this passage and the descending scale.

Example 12. Fenaroli, Fugue no. 1, mm. 23-30: hidden entries realized, with added staff showing the correspondence with the "Rule of the Octave".

Playing this bass, the right hand of any well-trained *partimento* player would almost automatically search for its complement, the chords of the "Rule of the Octave", which—with insignificant changes—correspond exactly to the subject of the fugue. The principle of complementarity applies here to the undisputed foundation of the entire *partimento* theory.

My next example shows another instance of this principle of complementarity. The subject of Fenaroli's Fugue 2 from book V is accompanied by another *fauxbourdon* (Example 13a). As usual, this *fauxbourdon* is not a countersubject, and therefore it will not appear in the bass as a signal for the presence of some hidden entry. To make things more difficult, this time the subject cannot be accompanied using the "Rule of the Octave". In fact, it does not have a scalar structure, but rather circles insistently around $\hat{3}$.

Example 13. (a) Fenaroli, Fugue no. 2 from Book V: Subject and fauxbourdon (mm. 1-11); (b) Graphic analysis of the subject; (c) counterpoint to subject and answer in mm. 33-43; (d) complementary elements in mm. 33-43.

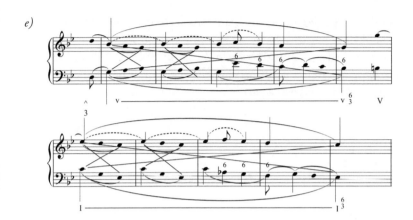

Example 13. (e) Graphic analysis of the "hidden" entries.

Example 13b gives a voice-leading analysis of the subject. The E flat is prolonged three times: the first time through a descending third progression, which is repeated immediately. The last, and larger prolongation uses a neighboring tone, F, followed by the final descent to D and C. The performer who wants to find the place where a hidden entry of this subject occurs, therefore, must scan the *partimento* for an element that might fit the subject and complement its harmonic and contrapuntal implications. This element is in the counterexposition in mm. 33-43, shown in Example 13c: it allows the setting of the answer and the subject (see Example 13d). As Example 13e shows, the coupling of the two elements in a complementary relation produces a prolongation through voice exchange by contrary motion (for the subject) and direct motion (for the answer). Notice also that the voice leading patterns are "nested": the same model (Eb–D–C in the top voice and C–G–Eb in the bass) appears as surface detail (repeated twice in the first two bars of the example) and on a larger span of music (see the notes connected with the beams).

The principle of complementarity governing the "hidden" thematic statements of subject and answer in a *partimento*-fugue is as follows: in order to be identified, the "hidden" entries must be part of a recognizable two-voice pattern (not necessarily in invertible counterpoint). The easiest patterns are those, such as the "Rule of the Octave," or the sequential bass patterns, that are also the fundamental schemes of the unfigured bass accompaniment Other patterns, like the voice exchange shown in Example 13, were obviously not identified as such at the time of Fenaroli. Still, their inclusion in *partimento* exercises confirms that the memorization of these patterns was considered as a part of composition pedagogy.

7.

CONCLUSIONS

The Neapolitan tradition of *partimento*-fugue continued well beyond the early nineteenth century. Like all other kinds of *partimento*, the fugues written by early and mid eighteenth century composers (such as Gaetano Greco, Leonardo Leo or Francesco Durante) gradually faded into oblivion. At the end of the nineteenth century the only *partimenti* still in use were those of Fenaroli and Zingarelli. About the mid nineteenth century, however, a new format of fugal exercises arose, the so-called *Basso imitato e fugato* (fugal and imitated bass). The first who composed them appears to be Pietro Raimondi, undisputably the greatest contrapuntist in 19th century Italy. Differently from the *partimento*-fugue, a *basso imitato e fugato* consists in a bass line only, and requires a written realization in open score (usually in four voices with the appropriate clefs). In these respects, it is more akin to the *disposizione* than to the *partimento*-fugue. This tradition continued with Pietro Platania, a student of Raimondi who inherited from his master the status of Italy's leading contrapuntist.[29]

In all its different facets, the *partimento*-fugue (and fugue in general) has been at the core of composition studies in Naples, and in Italy, for more than two centuries. In a famous letter to Francesco Florimo, written in 1871, Giuseppe Verdi stated that during his studies with Vincenzo Lavigna (a student of Fenaroli) he "did nothing other than canons and fugues, fugues and canons of all sorts".[30]

---

29. On the Raimondi tradition see Gaetano Stella, "Partimenti in the Age of Romanticism: Raimondi, Platania, and Boucheron," in: *Journal of Music Theory* 51/1 (2007), pp. 161–186.
30. Quoted in Roberta Montemorra Marvin, "Verdi learns to compose: the writings of Bonifazio Asioli," in: *Studi musicali* 36/2 (2007), p. 439.

As the present volume demonstrates, the legacy of the Neapolitan school of composition, with its breadth and richness, is now being revived by a growing circle of scholars and musicians. It is to be hoped that the principles behind it might continue to serve the education of musicians, as they have done for such a long time.

THE PLAYING OF *PARTIMENTO*

COMPREHENSIVE TRAINING
FOR THE COMPOSING AND
IMPROVISING INTERPRETER

Rudolf Lutz

Thanks to detailed studies of the *partimento* as a training method in eighteenth- and nineteenth-century Italy, in recent years much light has been shed on, and many discoveries made about this widespread teaching method. First and foremost I would like to mention the work of Robert Gjerdingen. He has made a large number of such *partimenti* accessible in the worldwide web.[1] The comments about the phenomenon in his treatment of the "Galant Style" — an essay that is most welcome for me as an improviser — demonstrate the importance of this training for budding *maestri di capella* and keyboardists.[2]

Thus, I would like to limit myself to a short description of this bass-oriented method, so that I can then go in more detail into the question of the extent to which the work with *partimenti* can be valuable for improvisational training. This will be demonstrated by means of specific exercises with commentaries.

---

1. Robert O. Gjerdingen, *Monuments of Partimenti — A Series Presenting the Great Collections of Instructional Music Intended for the Training of European Court Musicians*, http://www.faculty-web.at.northwestern.edu/music/gjerdingen/partimenti/index.htm, accessed 9 May 2009.
2. Robert O. Gjerdingen, *Music in the Galant Style — Being an Essay on Various Schemata Characteristic of Eighteenth-Century Music for Courtly Chambers, Chapels, and Theaters, Including Tasteful Passages of Music Drawn from Most Excellent Chapel Masters in the Employ of Noble and Noteworthy Personages, Said Music All Collected for the Reader's Delectation on the World Wide Web*, New York 2007.

1.

THE *PARTIMENTO*

The *partimento* is part of a composition, usually the bass, or at least
the outline of the bass. In some cases this is provided with figures
(i.e. figured bass), but often can be managed without. Now and again
suitable motives are annotated. We also find contrapuntal works,
called *partimento*-fugues. A musical work must be produced from
these basses, i.e. missing voices must be invented, or perhaps most
aptly "found". This concerns the usually two or at most three upper
voices, which are initiated by the bass. This activity can be compared
to a puzzle: which bass progressions, usually of two or more notes,
can be recognized and performed as part of a harmonic structure?
The results, which one could call models or modules, form the basis
of a musical epoch. The models, and in particular their realization,
change(s) according to the style. (From a rhetorical point of view,
their *decoratio*.) It is a lesson in stylistic nuclei, in harmonic/melodic
realization, but also a tutor in accompaniment, counterpoint, line,
and keyboard technique.

The *maestro* wrote a personal workbook for his students, with
exercises that were continuously adapted, from simple cadences to
complex bass passages. This workbook was called a *zibaldone*, meaning something like "noted unsystematically in a book", which was
certainly not the case with a good *maestro*. He would, in fact, recognize which exercises did not yet work naturally for his pupil, and so
at short notice he would repeatedly incorporate the same problems
in a new piece, such that in time his trusted student could set down
and play the progressions without hesitation. Of course entire collections of *partimenti* would be copied by the trainees and passed
on. Such collections can be traced back over decades. Indeed it can
be shown that the same *partimenti* were used to educate generations
of conservatory students.

One of the most notable *zibaldones* forms a supplementary volume to the new Mozart edition: the studies for Thomas Attwood.[3]
In these studies we find many exercises in figured bass, and harmony
and counterpoint, but also preliminary studies for composition.

---

3. Erich Hetzmann, Cecil B. Oldman, Daniel Heartz & Alfred Mann (eds.), *Thomas
Attwoods Theorie und Kompositionsstudien bei Mozart*, Kassel 1965.

Mozart's thorough development and his wonderful corrections of Attwood's solutions are most impressive.

In short, one can say that working on musical correspondences with *partimenti* meant a comprehensive education, which both led to insight into theoretical aspects and promoted technical playing skills (particularly on the keyboard), and set the compositional standards which were revered at the leading courts.

2.
TRAINING IN HISTORICAL IMPROVISATION
AT THE SCHOLA CANTORUM BASILIENSIS

In our training program for improvisation at the *Schola Cantorum Basiliensis*, work with *partimenti* and the playing of *partimenti* (so-called *partimentieren*) has been cultivated in our training for keyboardists with great success since around 1994.[4] Work with *partimenti* also allows us to transmit the art of improvisation to monodists, not only in groups, but also as soloists.

In addition to numerous basses, the historical collections contain initial explanations of elementary aspects of musical teaching such as the names of notes, instruction about solmization and the handling of dissonances, and the fundamentals of figured bass.[5]

Example 1. Giuseppe A. Pastore (ed.), Francesco Durante: Bassi e fughe — un manuale inedito per riscoprire la vera prassi esecutiva della Scuola napoletana del Settecento, *Padova 2003, p. 3.*

---

4. See 2.7 below.

5. Giuseppe A. Pastore (ed.), *Francesco Durante: Bassi e fughe — un manuale inedito per riscoprire la vera prassi esecutiva della Scuola napoletana del Settecento*, Padova 2003.

2.1 *OSTINATI*

In Basel we often start the improvisational training with work on *ostinato* bass models. These are developed from figured bass, with voice leading given particular weight. Simultaneous training with teachers of figured bass produces important synergies and allows insights from different viewpoints.

Example 2. Phrygian cadence/half-close in minor/lamento bass.

Example 2 displays the *partimento* system in ideal-typical fashion.

To the bass voice (a) is added a twin voice (b) (gymel) in thirds. The third voice is the *lamento* voice (c). It is a held voice, which becomes a seventh on the third bass note and resolves stepwise downwards in the manner of a 7–6 suspension. (The 6 on the bass note 2 becomes the 7 on the bass note 3. Here can be demonstrated on the one hand the introduction of dissonances and on the other, the treatment of dissonances.)

In the improvisatory work, one then works with these three voices.

- It is possible to invert the two upper voices in the sense of double counterpoint at the octave.
- The practice of diminution is applied to the three voices, i.e. the individual melodic steps (horizontal intervals) are ornamented in different subdivisions. This type of diminution can be played on a keyboard (organ, harpsichord, clavichord), as well as on a melodic or plucked instrument. I often use different colors for the individual voices to make them more easily recognizable.
- Different registers (tessituras) offer alternatives. These can be reached by means of transition passages and leaps, as is made clear in Example 3.

Example 3.[6]

The introduction of a fourth voice can be a next step (Ex. 4). This fourth voice is not always easy to set. The use of leaps, unisons, and voice exchange can be learnt practically and theoretically from these exercises.

Example 4.

I advise notating the melody lines — indicated in Example 5 with white, black, and triangular note symbols — in a diagram. In this way the voice leading of the main voices can be clearly identified, without needing to produce a score. (The "Guide Lines", a term from jazz methodology for monodists!)

Quartfall

Example 5.

---

6. Examples given without reference to historical works are exercises written by the present author.

Leaping from one line to another is introduced next (Ex. 6). This is always possible when a note is consonant with the bass. Dissonances must be handled linearly and their need for resolution honored. Here too we are dealing with cover for the bass, that is to say the extension of the *partimento* from the bass, from a technical/compositional as well as from a practical point of view.

Example 6.

The sounding together of the individual voices produces a harmonic progression, which can be denoted with chord symbols, figured bass, steps and functions. With the arpeggiation of these chords (this harmony), a further structural realization can be employed (Example 7).

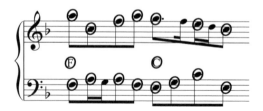

Example 7.

By means of these individual steps, the improviser / composer / player of figured bass is presented with the basic tools needed to produce an individual voice, which is distinguished by differentiated formation of the register, the effect (of each expression), the prosody (the formation of accents and phrases), and is consistent with the rules of voice leading. With this, working with *partimenti* is already described in essence.

2.2 A GREAT NUMBER OF DIFFERENT *OSTINATI*

In the course of the training program, further *ostinati* are dealt with in the above manner. These bass sequences highlight the fundamental models of the epoch and repeat, partly in a different context, the passages previously learnt. By means of the consecutive, varied repetition of the *ostinato* in the form of a *chaconne* or *passacaglia*, a complete form can be developed. Questions of contrast, intensification and *Fortspinnung* (continuous development) can be discussed, as can questions as to the number of voices, transitional passages and breaks (incisions). Examples from the literature are analyzed and these insights are incorporated in turn into the individual's work. A cycle results between production, performance and analysis. Music is conveyed and performed in an integral manner.

The improvisational, i.e. immediate command of this basic technique is like the verbal command of the grammatical and syntactical rules of a language. In language lessons, too, a verbal-improvised relationship with the language has a beneficial effect. Whoever has learnt to survive in a language in the corresponding country, will have gained — if accompanied by careful study of the relevant literature and grammar — a comprehensive linguistic ability. Stylistic aspects are studied in the light of continuous analyses, and over time a personal style develops in the particular "language". In this, a personal style can develop, which is in essence the individual arrangement of the parameters of an epoch.

The advantage of the work with these *ostinati* described above (in actual fact one could speak of a short *partimento*) is the fact that even with beginners one can work in musically artful dimensions. Musical phenomena are not only discussed, but above all worked with, which brings with it a welcome comprehension of theoretical and practical aspects.

If one peruses the rich *partimento* collections, the great number of exercises is striking. In all probability this is bound up with a pedagogical observation: the attainment of skill in the quick realization of such bass models necessitates a great deal of experience. Practice makes the master; a truism, which carries particular significance in this field.

2.3 DESCRIPTION OF FURTHER BASS MODELS

In the course of the training program, longer basses, each with specific problems and also with new technical demands must be "solved". These cases also concern the implied upper voices, which — as mentioned in the introduction — like in a crossword puzzle are only hinted at, and must be found.

Example 8.

In Example 8 there is a 2/4–6 chain. This shows some typical characteristics:
– the stepwise downward moving bass with syncopations
  and ligatures
– the typical figuring, which leads to the following realization:

Example 9.

If figures are lacking in later examples (consciously left out by the *maestro*), the attentive pupil will remember the 2/4–6 chain and "find" and employ it, even without figures.

An exercise, which leads efficiently to the "correct" lines and at the same time also to successful execution, is the following:

For myself as a teacher and also for my students, I take the bass of a master, e.g. the bass line of a trio sonata by Corelli. This is worked on in improvisatory fashion, the major lines searched out, two upper voices determined, written and then compared to Corelli's realization. Thereby important insights are gained, which can be utilized in one's own exercises. The beauty and elegance of the original solutions is more strikingly apparent than by their analysis.

Example 10. Arcangelo Corelli, Sonata Prima, Preludio, from Sonate à tre composte per L'Accademia dell'Em.mo e Rev.mo Sig.r Cardinale Otthoboni et all'Eminenza sua consecrate daArcangelo Corelli da Fusignano Opera Quarta, In Roma, 1694; *modern edition by J. Stenzl, Laaber 1986, p. 81.*

In Example 10 there is a rhythmization, which essentially leads to an individualization (decoration) of the bass line (disposition). Some elegant superpositions and the leaps of the voices in measure 3 are striking. In measure 4, the sixth in the 2nd violin part on the fourth beat of m. 3 becomes a seventh as a result of the bass step; well prepared, it swings over the *cantizans* to the *ultima*. Students stop short here; they grasp what a *cantizans* and an *ultima* are, though, if these terms have not already been introduced and explained earlier.

After this, new model examples, as well as well-trodden steps (sequences, progressions, 7–6 chains, cycles of falling fifths, cadences etc.) are worked on. The selection is the job of an experienced maestro, who himself writes, improvises, knows the style and therefore knows where and when which model can aid the progress of a student. Here again, the importance of a personal *zibaldone* cannot be overestimated. If the same epoch is dealt with in figured bass and chamber music classes, satisfying and extremely instructive insights will usually be gained. Whoever recognizes a model as an entity and immediately knows how to realize the most beautiful voice leading, is skilful in the realization of a bass. Sight-reading, but also the understanding of the logic and the phrase is improved. Without much ado, difficult bass passages, fiddly runs, trills and figures can be incorporated, which promote good keyboard technique.

In what follows, other models will not be given, but instead, something will be said about the introduction of figures.

2.4 FIGURES AND MOTIVES

Durante gives the following entry:

Example 11. Giuseppe A. Pastore (ed.), Francesco Durante: Bassi e fughe — un manuale inedito per riscoprire la vera prassi esecutiva della Scuola napoletana del Settecento, *Padova 2003, p. 176.*

In the minims in the bass passage, which prove to be leading notes, three different figures, motives, and melodic realizations can be incorporated according to the models (*Primo Modo, Secondo Modo, Terzo Modo*). Students locate the semitones and incorporate the appropriate motive at these points. This figure is one of a wide range of figures typical of the epoch and shapes the style in this manner. In this way, a formal overview and also motivic work can be learnt. As it is once again the maestro who anticipates the stock of figures that are incorporated at various points in the piece and conveys them to the students. It is clear yet again how great the influence of the teacher can be. In this case too, it can only work with dozens of such exercises.

2.5 COUNTERPOINT

Counterpoint is also learnt with exercises in *partimento.*

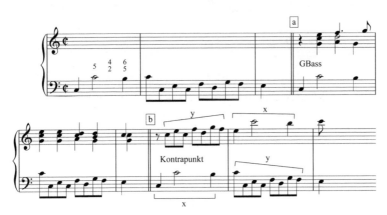

Example 12.

The bass can be presented, of course, with figures (see a), but also as double counterpoint at the octave (b).

Even fugues can be constructed using the *partimento* method. Here are two examples — from Handel's fugue tutor (Example 13) and from the Langloz manuscript (Example 14).

Example 13. A. Mann (ed.), G.F. Händel, Aufzeichnungen zur Kompositionslehre aus den Handschriften im Fitzwilliam Museum Cambridge, *Kassel 1978, p. 46.*

Example 14. William Renwick (ed.), The Langloz manuscript: fugal improvisation through figured bass, *Oxford 2001, p. 87.*

I let my advanced students write their own *partimento* fugues and studies in counterpoint. This activity promotes a command of the disposition and structure (of the harmony), and the result demonstrates the student's improved understanding of what has been learnt. The question is often posed what composition has to do with improvisation. I think: a great deal. For to my mind it is true that improvisation is a spontaneous flow of musical thoughts; a composition, the well thought-out compilation of different components. However, both are linked by a shared syntactical, grammatical, rhetorical, and structural linguistic environment. If the improvising musician is in danger of becoming ever more involved in his effective clichés, the composing musician can try to find an extension of the language by means of reflection and careful weighing up. Just as improvised music is influenced by the hand, the breath, and the throat, the head can play a larger part in composition. They both influence each other. If the compositions are learned and performed successfully, even transposed, new musical knowledge flows into the hand, the throat and the breath. The analysis of composed works of the period opens up, from the other side, their great effect.

Das XII. Kapitel.

Von Allemanden, Couranten, Sarabanden, Menuetten und Giquen, wie selbige aus einem schlechten General-Baß zu erfinden sind.

§. 1.

Wollen wir nun weiter gehen/ und aus vorgesetztem Baß eine Allemande zuwege bringen/ so wird nöthig seyn/ selbigen in zwo Reprisen einzutheilen/ damit bey dem ersten Absatz in der Quinta Modi geschlossen werde. Nun ist der Modus C; derohalben muß die Cadentz ins G kommen. Dieses ist bey allen (r) zu observiren/ wo 2. Reprisen vorfallen. So würde denn der Allemanden-Baß aussehen:

* probably e

Sarabanden-
Baß:

Example 15. Friedrich Erhardt Niedt, Musikalische Handleitung, *Hamburg 1710–17; reprints of the second edition (parts 1–2) and the posthumous edition (part 3), Hildersheim 2003, Ch. XI, p. 117.*

2.6. NIEDT: MUSICAL *MANUDUCTIO*

How all sorts of preludes, chaconnes, allemandes [...] can be found in a 'bad' figured bass.[7]

Here, too, we find an approach according to *partimento*. Niedt shows how the basis for movements of a suite, preludes, even chaconnes can be found in a two-part figured bass, which modulates from C to G, to e minor, and back again. By shifting the harmonic

---

7. Friedrich Erhardt Niedt, *Musikalische Handleitung*, Hamburg 1710–17; reprints of the second edition (parts 1–2) and the posthumous edition (part 3), Hildersheim 2003, Ch. XI, p. 117.

tempo of the action — the type of bar can be changed, the length of the individual bass notes made to fit the typical bar structure of a type of movement — a bass passage is individualized and changed (Ex. 15).

Niedt's technique also requires careful study, and it usually necessitates the assistance of the maestro before a student can utilize this "Niedtsian" technique of structural change in the bass. In the course of this development, students will work with many different models — of harmonic and melodic type — allow them to flow into their repertoire and, with time, be able to improvise meaningful, stylistically convincing music even without bass models.

2.7 THE PLAYING OF *PARTIMENTO*

The playing of *partimento* is a separate exercise — at any rate I have no knowledge of historical models. To this end I take a piece from the repertoire to be studied.

From this piece I extract a suitable bass line with corresponding figures. The bass is thus "de-individualized". Then I perform the bass as a figured bass, seek out the voice leading and get used to the progression. After that, a new realization can be found, and perhaps a new time signature, a new motive, a new effect introduced. Thus I transform the Allemande by Händel into an organ prelude or a sarabande. (In this, I am aided by Niedt's approach, with its shifting of the harmonic/melodic stages of the basic bass.)

I produce new runs, can transform these into multifarious pieces, and have many new works in every conceivable character at my disposal — for use during the playing of a church service, for example. In the interpretation of a work, the playing of *partimento* can shed much light on phrasing and give accents. The overall shape of a *partimento* is often easier to determine than that of a complex polyphonic structure.

Example 16. G. F. Händel, Suite in d minor, Allemande, from Acht grosse Suiten; *modern edition by R. Steglich, Kassel 1955.*

3.
CONCLUSION

A consideration of the nucleus of a type of music — in the epoch of figured bass most certainly the bass; in music of medieval and also of renaissance character more likely the Gregorian tenor — gives considerable insight into the particular period. The elaboration of this part of the music, *partimento,* can give us a comprehensive way in. A combination of theoretical and practical insights is attained. The composer, the director of music, the keyboardist, the orchestral musician and the monodic soloist all find here a form of training, which can transmit wide horizons and deep insight — for students and performers alike.

Translated from the German by Dr Jessica Horsley

THOMAS CHRISTENSEN

THOMAS CHRISTENSEN received a Ph.D. in Music Theory from Yale University in 1985. He taught at Vassar College, the University of Pennsylvania, the University of Iowa, and is currently professor of music and the humanities at the University of Chicago. His scholarly research centers on the history of music theory, with special interests in 18th-century intellectual history, problems in tonal theory, historiography, and aesthetics. He is the author of numerous books and articles, including a book on *Rameau and Musical Thought in the Enlightenment*, and was the general editor of the *Cambridge History of Western Music*.

ROBERT GJERDINGEN

ROBERT GJERDINGEN took his Ph.D. in Music History and Theory from the University of Pennsylvania in 1984. He held teaching positions at Carleton College, Harvard University and SUNY at Stony Brook, among others, and is currently professor of music theory and cognition at Northwestern University. He is the author of numerous books, articles and reviews in the fields of music theory, music perception and 18th-century musical style, among them his book on *Music in the Galant Style*. He is also the editor of the online collection *Monuments of Partimenti* and is currently working on a similar collection of *Monuments of Solfeggi*.

Personalia

GIORGIO SANGUINETTI

GIORGIO SANGUINETTI studied piano at the Conservatory of
Milan, composition at the conservatory of Pesaro and Schenkerian
analysis with Carl Schachter at Mannes College. He worked as a con-
cert pianist, taught piano at various Italian conservatories and gave
music theory classes at the University of Calabria, the Conservatory
of Milan and City University New York. Since 2002 he is Associate
Professor at the University of Rome 'Tor Vergata'. His research
fields include: History of Italian theory, Schenkerian analysis, Opera
analysis and post-tonal theory. He is currently working at a book on
The Art of Partimento. History, Theory and Practice in Naples.

RUDOLF LUTZ

RUDOLF LUTZ has been organist at St. Laurenzen, the protestant
city church of St. Gallen, since 1973 and has significantly influenced
and impacted its musical live. He was furthermore chief conductor
in charge of the St. Gallen Bach-Choir from 1986 to 2008, the St.
Gallen Chamber ensemble from 1986 to 2010 and finally lecturer
at the respective university of music in Basel (Schola Cantorum
Basiliensis). Since 2006 he is the artistic director of the J.S.Bach
Foundation in St. Gallen.

EDITORS
Dirk Moelants
Kathleen Snyers

SERIES EDITOR
Peter Dejans

AUTHORS
Thomas Christensen
Robert Gjerdingen
Giorgio Sanguinetti
Rudolf Lutz

LAY-OUT
Wilfrieda Paessens, Ghent

PRESS
Bioset, 100gr

ISBN 978 90 5867 828 7
D/2010/1869/35
NUR 663

© 2010 by Leuven University Press /
Universitaire Pers Leuven / Presses Universitaires de Louvain
Minderbroedersstraat 4, B-3000 Leuven (Belgium)

#1   INTER DISCIPLINAS ARS
Michel Butor, Henri Pousseur, Herman Sabbe,
Silvio Senn

Inter Disciplinas Ars contains four reflections on music from a multidisciplinary approach: literature, Music pedagogy, Music sociologie and filosophy
ISBN 9061869293 – 1998
Also available in Dutch: Inter Disciplinas Ars (ISBN 906186917x)

#2   THEORY INTO PRACTICE
Composition, Performance and Listening Experience
Nicholas Cook, Peter Johnson, Hans Zender

The central theme of this book is the relationship between the reflections about and the realization of a musical composition.
ISBN 9061869943 – 1999
Also available in Dutch: Theorie in Praktijk.Compositie, uitvoering en luister-ervaring (ISBN 9061869935)

#3   CAHIER « M »
A brief Morphology of Electric Sound.
Dick Raaijmakers

CAHIER-M is about the morphology of electric sound. Particular attention is given to the morphological relationship between the typically uniform nature of electric sound and the multi-layered sound structures used by post-WWII serial composers.
ISBN 9058670759 – 2005 (reprint)
Also available in Dutch: Cahier « M ». Kleine Morfologie van de elektrische klank. (ISBN 9058670767)

#4 ORDER AND DISORDER
Music-Theoretical Strategies in 20th-Century Music
Jonathan Dunsby, Joseph N. Strauss, Yves Knockaert,
Max Paddison, Konrad Boehmer

Order and Disorder discusses theoretical, historical and
philosophical aspects of music and theory after the 1950s in
relation to performance practice.
ISBN 9058673693 – 2004

#5 IDENTITY AND DIFFERENCE
Essays on Music, Language and Time
Jonathan Cross, Jonathan Harvey, Helmut
Lachenmann, Albrecht Wellmer, Richard Klein

Identity and Difference collects five writings on the relationship between music and language and music and time, both
from the view of composers, musicologists, critics, philoso-
phers and music theorists.
ISBN 9058674134 – 2004

#6 TOWARDS TONALITY
Aspects of Baroque Music Theory
Thomas Christensen, Penelope Gouk, Gérard Geay,
Susan McClary, Markus Jans, Joel Lester, Marc
Vanscheeuwijck

Towards Tonality considers the often complex connections
and intersections between, e.g., modal and tonal idioms,
contrapuntal and harmonic organisation, etc. from various
perspectives as to the transition (towards tonality) from the
Renaissance to the Baroque era.
ISBN 9789058675873 – 2007

#7   NEW PATHS
Aspects of Music Theory and Aesthetics in the Age of
Romanticism
*John Neubauer, Janet Schmalfeldt, Scott Burnham,
Susan Youens, Jim Samson*

New Paths focuses on a broad range of issues on nineteenth century music in a re-contextualising and fresh manner: the concept of organicism, the musical evolution of
Beethovens 'Bridgetower' Sonata, the staging of subjectivity
in Beethoven's late music, Franz Lachner and the limits of the
Lied and the environmental influences on Chopins work.
ISBN 9789058677341 – 2009

#8   UNFOLDING TIME
Studies in Temporality in Twentieth Century Music
*Bruce Brubaker, Pascal Decroupet, Mark Delaere,
Justin London, Ian Pace*

For performers, the primary perception of music is arguably
the way in which it unfolds in 'real time'; while for composers
a work appears 'whole and entire', with the presence of the
score having the potential to compress, and even eliminate,
the perception of time as 'passing'. The paradoxical relationship between these two perspectives, and the subtle media-
tions at the interface between them, form the subject matter
of this collection of studies.
ISBN 9789058677358 – 2009

03. **Dynamics of Constraints**
    Essays on Notation, Editing and Performance
    Mieko Kanno, Paulo de Assis, Juan Parra Cancino

Expresses some fundamental issues addressed by ORCiM's research group 'the musician's relation to notation'. Paulo de Assis argues that critical editions should generate critical users, advocating for a new kind of editor and performer; Mieko Kanno's contribution reflects the rapid expansion of the use of electronics in contemporary music, while Juan Parra Cancino points towards a kind of composition, where both the performing and the listening experience don't aim to achieve a 'final' version of the piece.

ISBN 9789490389024 – 2009

Both series are available at University Press Leuven: **www.upers.kuleuven.be**